THE

DIVINE HUMAN

IN

THE SCRIPTURES.

BY

TAYLER LEWIS,

UNION COLLEGE.

ὁ Λόγος τοῦ Θεοῦ ζῶν καί ἐνεργής. . . . HEB. iv : 12.

ὁ Λόγος σὰρξ ἐγένετο. . . . JOHN i : 14.

NEW YORK:
ROBERT CARTER AND BROTHERS,
No. 530 BROADWAY.

1860.

EDWARD O. JENKINS,
Printer & Stereotyper,
No. 26 Frankfort Street.

PREFACE.

A TRUE faith in the Scriptures must have its strength in the Scriptures themselves. This would seem to be a proposition of the clearest reason. If the Bible be the *word* of God with a *human voice*, then must it speak to the human soul directly as no other word, no other voice, can speak. Too much have we relied on outward helps. Not casting away, then, but leaving behind our Apologies for the Bible, our Philosophies of the Bible, our Reconciliations of the Bible with Science, we should come directly to the Scriptures, with the rational as well as reverent belief, that if they are divine they must contain within themselves their own strong self-evidencing power. We would say to the young man disturbed with scepticism, Read your Bible. We would say to all who have difficulties which they honestly wish removed, Study the Scriptures, meditate therein by day and by night—

Nocturna versate manu, versate diurna.

It is the only true and lasting cure of scepticism, whether for an individual or an age. It might be thought that there is some risk in the prescription, and doubtless it may be so with its first effects; for the difficulties and stumbling-blocks may show themselves before the deep verities have begun to arrest and amaze the soul: but let there be perseverance, and the divine medicine will reveal its power; "the sun of righteousness will at length arise with *healing* in its wings."

At no time, we believe, are such thoughts more important

than at present. Faith is weakened by habitual reliance upon outward props, even when sound. The age, and all serious minds of the age, are called to the inward study of the *word* itself. In the signs of the times we seem to hear the voice that came to Augustine in his memorable conversion-struggle in the garden, "Take up the book and read—take up the book and read." It seems to say to us with a new emphasis, Ερευνᾶτε τὰς γραφάς, "Search the Scriptures," explore the Scriptures, there are hidden treasures there, there are living waters there; study the Scriptures, they contain more than *knowledge*, the words they speak unto you, "they are *spirit* and they are *life*."

The above thoughts are not made directly the subject of the following book, but they suggestively pervade it, and may, therefore, justly occupy its prefatory page.

The writer would merely add, that the present volume has grown out of what was intended as an introduction to another work on the Figurative Language of the Scriptures, and which, with the divine permission, he hopes soon to give to the public. Some of the thoughts in such intended introduction were deemed worthy of being treated at greater length, and with more liberty. Hence the expansion which has resulted in the book here offered to the Church. It is hoped that it will be found to occupy that ground of our common Christianity which carries us above all narrow sectarianism. Whatever may be its defects, in other respects, it is believed to be evangelical, churchly, catholic in that true sense of catholicism which is acknowledged by all true believers.

CONTENTS.

CHAPTER I.

CHAPTER II.

CHAPTER III.

CHAPTER IV.

CHAPTER V.

CHAPTER VI.

CHAPTER VII.

CHAPTER VIII.

CHAPTER IX.

CHAPTER X.

CHAPTER XI.

CHAPTER XII.

CHAPTER XIII.

CHAPTER XIV.

CHAPTER XV.

CHAPTER XVI.

CHAPTER XVII.

CHAPTER XVIII.

CHAPTER XIX.

CHAPTER XX.

ERRATA.

Page 194, line 8, for *Gibreh* read *Gibeah*.

" 175, " 1, for דירך " דורך

" 238, " 21, for אקֹק " אֹתֹת

THE

DIVINE HUMAN

IN THE SCRIPTURES.

CHAPTER I.

THE WORD—How used in Scripture—Written—Incarnate—The Perfect Analogy—The Word of Truth—The Word of Life—The Term, "Son of Man"—The Pure Humanity of Christ—No Man ever so Human—The Humanity of the Written Word—Analogy in the Conception and Formation of each—The Divine in the Human—All Revelation Anthropopathic, whether in the Flesh or in Language.

THE WRITTEN WORD—THE INCARNATE WORD. It is no mere fanciful or verbal analogy that connects these two ideas. This is shown by the fact that there are passages of Scripture where it is difficult to distinguish between them, or to determine with certainty that one of them is the *exclusive* sense, or that both are not comprehended in one essential and inseparable significance. There is the *Λόγος Ἀληθείας*, and the *Λόγος Ζωῆς*, the Word of Truth, and the Word of Life. "Of his will he begat us through the *word of truth.*" Is it the written word here, that is, the truth conveyed in it as presented to the mind, or is it "the Word that became flesh," Christ in the soul, not as truth merely, but as a living power? the *Word of Truth*, the *true Word*—by a well-known Hebraism so common in the New Testament—the *true Word* in the sense of the *real Word*, the *living Word*, the ἔμφυτος λόγος, or *in-growing Word.* So, also, "Sanctify them through thy truth, thy Word is truth." It is the rationalist's favorite text. In interpreting it he thinks only of truth, as the food of the intellect, and that, too, not always as Bible truth, but truth in general, reason, doctrine, knowledge, as the regenerating, soul-nurturing, sanctifying power. So is it most commonly taken, even by the soberest theologians; but it is far from being certain that this is the right interpretation, or, at least, the only true interpretation of the language. It was not the favorite interpretation of the early Church ; it has not been the interpretation, at least the exclusive interpretation, of the most spiritually-minded in later times. "Sanctify them," consecrate them, set them apart, *in thy truth*, *ἐν τῇ ἀληθεία σου*. It may be doubted whether *ἐν* is instrumental here, as commonly taken, or does not have a deeper significance, as in that inexhaustible language, *εν πνεύματι, ἐν Χριστῷ*. "Sanctify them in thy truth," says the Redeemer, and then, as though to guard against human misapprehension of this intercessory pleading, the sentence is added, "Thy Word," *ὁ Λόγος ὁ σός*, the Word that is thine, the Word that pre-eminently represents the Infinite Father, the "Image of the Invisible God," the Incarnate Word, *that* "is the truth," the sanctifying truth, or the true sanctifying Word, by union to which men become holy, separate from the world, united to God, and "partakers of the Divine nature." It is the Word of Truth, or the true Word, not as a dogma, a thought, an intellectual verity, though in relation to the highest and most religious things, but an indwelling, energizing presence,—truth alive in the soul, entering into and constitutive of its very being. The other—the rationalistic or dogmatic view—has also its evidence. The affirmation of the one aspect is not the denial of the other. Both may be united; both may be regarded as inseparable parts of one idea, or the manifestation of the infinite in the finite; for the highest truth we have is anthropopathic; it is a representation to the sense, and in sense-conceptions, of the ineffable and the eternal that can be received in no other way. Thus it is that the *Word of Truth* and the *Word of Life* may be regarded as essentially connected; but certainly, if we attempt to separate them logically in our minds, as we may do, care should be taken not to convert the living aspect into the figure, and make the naked, abstract truth the higher and more powerful reality.

The *Written*, the *Incarnate Word.* It may be called analogy, but the analogy, the proportion, is perfect. As the divine to the human nature in Christ, so is the divine thought, the divine life in the Scriptures, to their human form. It is perfect in kind, perfect in degree ; it is analogous, *ἄνα λόγον*, throughout. In both we have the infinite in the finite, the divine in the human, the ineffable in the forms of sense, the essential as exhibited in the phenomenal,—the absolute, the eternal, the unconditioned as represented in the relative, the temporal, the flowing images of time and space. So in degree ; the thought is carried to its ultimate in each. Christ is not only human, but most intensely human. Never was there a man so purely man as this "second man, the Lord from heaven." Never man spake so humanly, felt so humanly, loved so humanly, lived so humanly, died so humanly. Bone of our bone, and flesh of our flesh, he had a purer humanity than any of the other sons of Adam, inasmuch as it was free from that demoniac adulteration which had been produced by sin. Hence is he so emphatically called, and so delights to call himself, the Son of Man. The term has more meaning than it seems at first view to possess. In the Syriac, the Saviour's native dialect, it is the name for humanity itself. *Bar nosho*, the *Son of Man*, is man generically; the filial part of the compound denoting the identity, and continuance, and purity of the generic idea. Hence is he appointed to judge humanity (John v., 27), "because he is the Son of Man." It is only from Christ's most perfect manhood that we rise to the best thought of his divinity. He could not have been so perfect a man, so complete in his finiteness, had he not been also divine and infinite. The mystery no mind can solve; the fact is not only most glorious for our apprehension, but the ground of all our hope. This is more fully dwelt upon in a subsequent chapter; it is here stated as an introductory or ground idea. And so of the written Word. The analogy is without a flaw. No book is so purely human as the Bible; there is no one in which the actors are so purely men. Its language, idioms, figures, are all addressed to our most intense, and therefore most universal humanity. This is proof of its divinity. Nothing but an inspiration in the human, breathing through it, penetrating and sounding every part of it, could have so brought out the human. Its language, therefore, whilst most intensely ours, is, of all language, the most divine. The philosophic or scientific styles of speech would have betrayed their purely earthly origin, by their partial, their one-sided, and therefore false anthropopathism; for it would have been anthropopathism still, though not the divine anthropopathism of the Scriptures. The very attempt to get above humanity would have produced a distorted and inhuman representation. The Scriptures, like Christ, come down to us—come down to us *perfectly;* they occupy the common plane of our nature. Hence their language, if inspired at all, is inspired throughout. The very words and figures are full of the divine breath, and are therefore to be searched for the divine thought, the divine emotion, that fills out this perfect humanity.

Thus, too, is the analogy perfect in respect to the conception and generation of both Words, or both these expressions of the divine in human form. Christ's humanity was conceived of the Holy Ghost, and born of the Virgin Mary. It was thus a true humanity, linked in its life-source with our humanity, and growing out of it. We can conceive of an artificial or mechanically-formed Christ,—if we may use the strange expression,—such as was fancied by some of the old heretics who denied the miraculous conception. We can think of a new being, made outwardly and inwardly like the human race—so like that sense and thinking could discover no difference—something like Agassiz's fancy in respect to separate Adams or centres of creation. But such a humanity, if we may call it so, would not have been our humanity. Such a being would not have been our brother, any more than an inhabitant of the remotest visible star. There would be no common point in time and space in which his life could be numerically one with ours, or ours one with his. There could have been no abiding generic unity. Such a human, we say, would not be our human. And so, on the other hand, can we conceive of an artificial written word, or a mechanical inspiration of the Scriptures. It might have been written on the sky, or, what would have been very much the same thing, by men employed, not as thinking, feeling, conceiving, in all their freedom as men, but as outwardly moved, as amanuenses or involuntary utterers. But this would not have been *our* Scriptures, our revelation, our most human as well as most divine book. It would not have been an inspiration *in* the human, and *through* the human. Its thought must link itself with our thought, its emotion with our emotion, as light from light, and life from life. Through the divine "o'ershadowing" power it is conceived in human feeling, nurtured in human thinking, fashioned in human imagery, and brought out at last in human language. Thus, as ultimate products, and through this linked series of generation, the very words are inspired, not merely the thoughts or emotions, as though these could be separated from the words. For how can there be feelings that do not fashion to themselves images, and how can there be images in the mind that do not arrange themselves in thoughts, and how can there be thoughts that do not take the form of words! The process is inseparable. The first inspiration, or inbreathing, has in it, not only virtually, but in design, all the rest. Thus the very words of Scripture are inspired. This is the great truth, the living truth, that forms the only basis of any hopeful interpretation. The language is what God meant it to be. It is his chosen method, his best method, for revealing himself to human minds. As the Infinite must be unknown, unthought, or clothe himself in the forms of the finite, so this is the form he has selected as the most human, the most perfect in its finiteness. He has taken this rather than the style of science and philosophy, even as Christ came in the purest and most universal humanity instead of that false anthropomorphism that might have been preferred by the more ambitious forms of human thought. Our philosophy may not like the word; there is none, perhaps, to which the common irreligious thinking affects to be more opposed; but we cannot escape from the thing itself; and why should we wish to escape from it? All religion, all revelation, is a divine anthropopathism. No other is conceivable. The Written Word, the Incarnate Word, however we may regard them as differing in rank, are analogous manifestations of the same condescension in the Infinite and Ineffable Personality.

CHAPTER II.

THE LANGUAGE OF THE BIBLE DIVINELY CHOSEN — Principle of Interpretation — "No Iota of the Law shall fail" — Patristic Interpretation — The Great Bible Thoughts, then new — The Fathers found them everywhere — The Modern View of the Scriptures as a Fragmentary Book — Traditional Interpretation — Christ in the Scriptures — The Hero-Messiah — Hieronymus and Matthew Henry — De Wette and Davidson — The Professional Scholiast and the true Homeric Interpreter — The Unity of the Scriptures — Modern Interpretation finds too little in them.

THE previous thoughts furnish the ground of a most important hermeneutical position. The canon and its preamble may be thus stated—*The language of the Bible is divinely chosen—its words and figures are designed to be just what they are; "eloquia Domini, eloquia casta, argentum igne examinatum, probatum terra, purgatum septuplum; the words of the Lord are pure words, like silver tried, seven times refined." We may therefore search them, and rationally search them, for a divine significance.* Not one jot or tittle of it shall fail to reward our study. Christ has given us assurance of this; the Light of the World hath told us that the Scriptures are every where full of *Him* and His salvation. He himself found rich meanings lying under words and forms of speech in which the Sadducean rationalists of his day saw nothing. We may, therefore, expect to discover in them "treasures new and old." We shall see "wondrous things out of the divine law," and these will be, not merely conceits of our own minds, but thoughts substantial, living ideas, having in themselves evidence that they are true fruits, not of any mere human thinking, but of the ἔμφυτος λόγος, the "*ingrowing* word," the *life-giving* word that *saves*, that is, *heals*, makes sound, our souls,—the *word* that co-essentiates itself with our spiritual life, in distinction from the knowledge that lies only in the sense and memory, or, at the utmost, only lodges in the chambers of the speculative intellect, instead of entering into the very growth of the spiritual constitution.

Interpretations grounded on such an idea may, indeed, be visionary. Although there is a divine warrant for thus studying the Scriptures, there is none for the individual human infallibility. Even as fancies, however, if they be but the fancies of a sanctified imagination, they may still have about them the holy fragrance of a true original inspired conception, and thus, in fact, be nearer the inner truthfulness, than many a more scientific exegesis to which, critically, no objection could be taken. This latter remark holds true of many an interpretation of the earlier Fathers that is held in contempt by the modern scholiast. The Cross, the Regeneration, the Church, the New Life, the Spiritual Temple, the New Humanity, the New Jerusalem or City of God,—these glorious ideas then so fresh and wonderful, together with their sacramental signs, they found in many a text where the modern exegesis finds them not, and where we are compelled to say, the modern exegesis is correct, dry, hard, and sometimes, even worthless, as it may seem to be. Thus Hieronymus, in his Commentaries, often finds in the Scriptures what is not there logically, or even metaphorically,—at least in the particular passage to which he assigns it. Yet even in such cases, the interpretation is but the vivid outgrowth of true Biblical ideas ; that is, of ideas that men would never have had without the Bible. They are living seeds sown in the souls of holy men from the "ingrowing word," and they come out every where, often irregularly and in wild luxuriance. The very extravagance of their germination shows, not only the fertility of the new soil, but the rich life that was in the original seminal power. Is it irrational to think that more of this true power of the word may be learned from minds in such a state than from the colder hermeneutics, even though the latter may give us the more correct interpretation of particular passages?

These great Bible thoughts, as we have said, were then new and wonderful. The shadows of them had been forecast from the sequestered Jewish religion, but their morning splendors were then just rising above the world's horizon. Hence it is not strange that these earliest Christian writers found them almost every where, lying under many a figure and prophecy where a cooler, and, perhaps, a less truly Bible-instructed imagination, fails to detect their appearance. There was to Christ a light in the Old Testament that the blinded Sadducee saw not. Paul had some key to the interpretation of the older Scripture utterly unknown to the rationalist, whether Jewish or Christian, and the use of which seems mystical even to true lovers of the Sacred Writings. And so these holy men, in the early days of the Christian life, had a method of interpretation which we should study closely before we venture rashly to reject it as wholly fanciful or absurd. Some of their errors are very obvious; we see very plainly where they were wrong ; and yet how often is even the coldest reader compelled to wonder at the exceeding aptness of the suggested thought, the strange coincidence of idea, although he himself, perhaps, would never have found it, never even suspected its existence.

Is there not some tenable ground lying between the free fancies of the earlier, and the exceeding dryness of the most modern interpretation? We think there is, and that the Christian mind will, ere long, find it. We must make more of the Scriptures, or give them up. One thing is certain: this rationalistic interpretation, so called, cannot long support a living Christianity. We say it even of the better kind, such as that of the school of Stuart, Davidson and others, for whom we feel all respect. Some of these are pious as well as learned men, but their piety was nurtured under a Scriptural training quite different from that which they are now introducing. The traditional interpretation of the Church, the *living word*, has entered into their spiritual growth, and they cannot wholly get rid of it. In others, who have had less or more of this old spiritual manna, the barrenness is becoming palpable and painful. The school of which we speak has great learning, and, in one sense, great value, but that value is only relative. It must rapidly depreciate unless regarded as subordinate to something else held in reserve. Without this, its philological interest, now its greatest charm, must soon give way to some superseding intellectual advance, and then there comes a soul-famine, or we must go back to the old traditional views of "Christ and his kingdom" as underlying all Scripture. We must revive that idea of which the Patristic exegesis is so full, and in which some contemned modern commentators, the "preaching commentators," as they are called, so greatly abound,—the idea of the Greater Temple, the higher spiritual house, that the Greater Son of David was to build for the Lord. We must take again, as the key of all right interpretation, that ancient myth, if any prefer to call it so, of the Hero Messiah, who is announced in the very beginning of Genesis, the suffering, warring, conquering Messiah, whose last great battle with the foe is so graphically described in the closing book of Revelations. It is all along one divine plan:

> *Θεοῦ δ' ἐτελείετο βουλή,*
> *ἐξ οὗ δή ταπρῶτα διαστήτην ἐρίσαντε.*

We trust it is not pedantic or irreverent to accommodate to the immeasurably higher idea this introductory language of the great heathen poet. "*The purpose of God has been ever receiving its accomplishment since the ancient day when they two first engaged in strife,*" the dark Power of Evil, and He who was to become the Woman's promised Seed, our Prince Immanuel, Son of Man, and Son of God—He of whom it is said that even from the beginning of earth's creation his "delight was with the children of Adam." It is, in fact this sacred βουλὴ ever receiving its fulfilment, that proves the Bible, with all its strange divisions into separate rhapsodies, as they may seem to some, to be indeed the work of one mind and on one great scheme. It is "the Book of the Wars of the Lord," of the great Theophanies, of the Supernatural in Humanity; it is the History of Redemption, no longer now the critics' fragmentary Iliad, but the most unique as it is immeasurably the grandest of epics.

"All things that are written in the Law, and in the Psalms, and in the Prophets concerning me, must be fulfilled." This was the ground of the Patristic interpretation. Such was the ground of all interpretation esteemed Christian until a very late period. The most undisputed tradition of the universal Church, the consent of Latin, Greek and Protestant exegesis, the verdict, we may say, of an eighteen hundred years Christianity, is not to be rashly set aside without risking the very idea of a supernatural revelation, and running into utter despair of any light from above.[1] If an idea so cardinal, so central, so catholic, is given up as false, where is there another in which we can expect to find the unity of the Bible, and without unity, who can believe it to be, in any sense, worth believing the Book of the Lord.

The interpretations of the Fathers may be often unbiblical in their special applications, and yet the product of a biblical spirit having, as a whole, a truer view of the mind of God and Christ in revelation than is entertained by the piece-meal critic who so proudly scorns what he is pleased to style their defective knowledge of hermeneutics. They do, indeed, often find Christ where he is not in the *words;* their boasting contemners do, doubtless, more frequently overlook him where he is really present in the *spirit.* We may admit that Hieronymus is often wrong, oftener, perhaps, than the interpreter of the modern school ; we may concede that Mathew Henry is less learned (so it is the fashion to speak of this humble Christian,) than De Wette or Davidson : still may we believe, on the deepest and most rational grounds, that both the Latin Father and the Puritan divine had really a closer communion, of thought as well as feeling, with the great Biblical ideas, and were, on this account, with all their errors, whether of knowledge or fancy, in the truest and profoundest sense, the best interpreters. The enthusiastic lover of Homer may often see in his favorite poet what the cooler scholiast disproves, and correctly disproves ; still we do not hesitate to maintain not only that our rhapsodist has more of the Homeric spirit but that he is also—in respect to all great and essential ideas—the best guide to the Homeric thought. The scholiast, or the more modern critic of a certain school, may have a keen eye for the digamma and the metrical hiatus, he may be sharp in scenting out anachronisms and supposed interpolations, he may bring out the best senses of some long hidden archaisms, he may clear up many an interesting matter of ancient custom, or of ancient geography; but the other has found more than this, even that without which all the rest is comparatively worthless, and to which the professional scholiast may be wholly blind; he has discovered in Homer that which makes him love him and study him intensely for his own sake, and not merely as a professional annotator who would be equally laborious and correct on any other ancient book in which there might be a similar professional interest. The wondrous bard has raised his whole soul to a higher sphere of thought; he is no longer the mere scholiast; he *believes* in Homer; and this faith carries him over all the difficulties that annotators have ever raised in respect to his matter or his text. Such enthusiastic admiration may have had, in some respects, a blinding effect; it may have produced a disposition to discover too much, or what may not really exist, but it has also led to that communion with the very soul of the great poet, to that interior thought or spiritual sense, as we may truly call it, without which scholia on Homer are of little more value than though they had been wasted on the most miserable of his Byzantine imitators.

We believe that this most modern interpretation is finding far too little in the Scriptures. Given by the divine mind, these holy books must have in them a depth and a fulness of meaning that the human intellect can never exhaust. If they are holy books, if they are *Sacræ Scripturæ*, as even the neologist conventionally styles them, then can there be thrown away upon them no amount of study, provided that study is ever chastened by a sanctified, truth-loving spirit, that rejoices more in the simplest teaching, and in the simplest method of teaching from God, than in the most lauded discoveries of any mere human science. Is it in truth the word of God—is it really God speaking to us? then the feeling and the conclusion which it necessitates are no hyperboles. We cannot go too far in our reverence, or in our expectation of knowledge surpassing in kind, if not in extent. The wisdom of the earth, of the seas, of the treasures hidden in the rocks and "all deep places," of the subterranean world, or of the stars afar off, brings us not so nigh the central truth of the Heavens, the very mind and thought of God, as one parable of Christ, or one of those grand prophetic figures through which the light of the infinite idea is converged, whilst, at the same time, its intensity is shaded for the tender human vision.

CHAPTER III.

Verbal Inspiration — How is it to be understood? — The Mechanical Theory — Inspiration through Human Emotions and Conceptions — The Divine in the Human throughout — The Last Product inspired as well as the First — In what Sense the Words and Figures sometimes more specially designed than the Thought itself — Trite Truths — Old Truths of the Conscience Recoined in new and striking Language — Difference between Moral and Scientific Truth — Extent or Comprehension sufficient in the one, Intensity demanded in the other — Algebraic Symbols — The Love and Wrath of God — The colder Ethical Language — Even this contains Figures, but they are dead—Illustrations — The Bare Formula, "God is averse to Sin," compared with the Burning Scriptural Language — The Tender Language of the Bible — Its Intense Humanity — Can the Infinite reveal Himself, at all, in Language?

It must, then, be one of the most unfaltering deductions of such a subdued spirit, thus believing in revelation as a fact as well as an idea, that not only its thought but its very language is divine. This one may hold without being driven to that extreme view of verbal inspiration which regards the sacred penmen as mere amanuenses, writing words and painting figures dictated to them by a power and an intelligence acting in a manner wholly extraneous to the laws of their own spirits, except so far as those laws are merely physical or mechanical. We may believe that such divine intelligence employed in this sacred work, not merely the hands of its media, not merely the vocal organs played upon by an outward material afflatus, not merely the mechanical impressions of the senses, or the more inward, though still outwardly reflected images of the fancy and the memory, but also the thoughts, the modes of thinking, modes of feeling, modes of conceiving, and, hence, of outward expression—in a word, the intellectual, emotional, and imaginative temperaments, all their own, each peculiar to the respective instruments, yet each directed, controlled, made holy, truthful, pure, as became the trustworthy agents for the time being, of so holy a work. The face is human, most distinctly human, yet each lineament, besides its own outward expression, represents also some part of that photographic process that had its origin in the world of light, and came down from "the Father of Lights," with whom there is no parallax or shadow of turning.

In this sense, the language, the very words, the very figures outwardly used, yea the etymological metaphors contained in the words, be they ever so interior, are all inspired. They are not merely general effects, in which sense all human utterances, and even all physical manifestations may be said to be inspired, but the specially designed products of *emotions* supernaturally inbreathed, these becoming outward in *thoughts*, and these, again, having their ultimate outward forms in *words* and *figures* as truly designed in the workings of this chain, and thus as truly inspired, as the thoughts of which these words are the express image, and the inspired emotions in which both thoughts and images had their birth. One theory of verbal inspiration begins with the language, as being that which is first and directly given to the inspired medium,—that is, given to him outwardly, by impressions on the organs of sense, or by some action on the sensorium, or in some mode, at least, that is outward to the most interior spirit; the other regards the supernatural action as beginning with the most interior spirituality, and ending with language as the last outward result. It is a product of a series, yet, as such product, representative of the entire spiritual action that has terminated in it, and having something corresponding to every step of such spiritual action in the whole course of its procession from the primal generative emotion to the ultimate sound or sign. It is all here, and a devout study of the language, aided by the spirit that gave it, will carry back the soul from the words to the images, from the images to the thoughts, from the thoughts to the spiritual emotion, or to communion with the *living word*, from whence the whole sacred stream has flowed. "*With thee is the fountain of life. In thy light do we see light. All the words of the Lord are pure; they are as choice silver tried; yea, seven times purified.*"

Throughout the process it is, indeed, the human soul energizing in its psychological order, and according to the law of its freedom, yet, from the very incipiency of the inspiration, purified, elevated, guarded and made unerring, by the power and presence of a higher spirit. The difference is a wide one, and yet this latter theory of verbal inspiration holds equally with the former that the very words are inspired; the peculiar language employed (and sometimes it is very peculiar and characteristic of the individual medium), the very figures, whether justified by the rules of ordinary criticism or not, are all chosen of God; they are "choice words," tried words, designed to be just what they are, and for special reasons *in themselves*, or their contexts, and not merely as connected with the general system of providential or natural means in the regulation of the universe. Like creation, it is a supernatural beginning, entering into and setting in motion a chain of sequences (natural if any choose to call them so) to bring out results which no previously created nature alone, whether old or new, would ever have produced. Thus regarded, the varied intellectual and emotional temperaments of Isaiah, of Ezekiel, of Paul, and John, are as directly made use of as the hands with which they write, the mouths with which they speak, or the Greek and Hebrew language they employ as the most outward vehicle of their thoughts and emotions.

In such a view of the matter we may even regard the figures, and the peculiar forms of language, and the emotions connected with them, as being, sometimes, even more the object of design than the bare thought itself,—that is, as having a greater share in the designed arrangements of the Divine communication. The thought is indeed the substance, but the manner of making it known, or, if already known, of impressing it on the human soul, may have been chiefly regarded in the selection of means for bringing out the written revelation. Much of the Scriptures consists of declarations of truths that have their seat already in the human conscience, of facts that are otherwise stored in the human traditional memory. In such cases the mode of impressing them upon the soul, so that they may sink into the interior life, in other words, of giving them moral power, becomes the chief thing. Trite truths are often the most valuable truths, though sometimes divested of force by their very *triteness.* They have been *worn,* as the word implies, and they must be recoined, sent anew to the mint, have a strong and deep *image* stamped upon the *idea,* that so the spiritual impression may be restored. Among other variety of media, God thus employs old truths themselves, as the instruments of a new revelation. This recoining is not by way of poetical hyperbole; for all language and all figures fall short of the intense reality of even an old and trite truth respecting God. Every power of human thought, or human imaging, is far below the strength demanded when there is an attempt to represent, worthily, the state or the attitude of the Eternal Mind toward moral good or evil. All such truths may be very old, uttered in the conscience, proclaimed through all history, and yet the thought, even as held by the inspired mind, immeasurably removed from the unspeakable, the inconceivable, reality. Logical abstractions here will not do at all, and as the ineffable idea cannot be conveyed to us in its essence or its vastness, the thought must be gathered, and condensed, and sent down to us through the converging lens of human emotions and human language, as feebly typical thereof.

Between moral truth and all other truth there is an essential difference that cannot be too much dwelt upon in our reasonings concerning a revelation and its language. It is a difference of altitude, we may say, in distinction from that of breadth or superficial quantity. Scientific or philosophic ideas, when *comprehended* in their *extent*, or numerical quantity of thought, if we may use the term, are the same for all comprehending minds. Moral ideas, on the other hand, have another element, namely, of *intensity*, which makes the same logical statement, with the same *logical* significance, an immensely different truth for different souls, or for the same soul at different times. It is only aside from this flowing element of intensity, or when it is taken as zero, that they become, like the ideas of science, the same for all intellects. Take, for example, the oldest and most common truth in theology or ethics, clothe it in the most general or least impassioned language, get words as far removed as possible from all personal or sense imagery: *Deity is averse to sin;* or, *Deity approves of the good.* It is, indeed, a tremendous truth in any language, but how different, we may say again, for different souls, or for the same soul in different moral states! Two men may be disputing about it; their logical language betrays no difference of abstract idea, it is perfectly consistent in every mode and figure through which they may choose to carry their polemics, and yet, could the soul of each be laid bare to the other they could not recognize each other's thought. Or, as an abstract proposition it might command the assent of two minds, and yet in what a different manner and measure may each receive, or lack, the life of the truth. To the one the logical terms *deity*, *aversion*, *sin*, are like the *dx dy* symbols of the mathematician; they are but *notions*, and they answer their logical or mathematical purposes equally well whatever *qauntities* these symbols represent; to the other, every term of the logical proposition, the subject, the predicate, the asserting copula even, are "words that breathe and thoughts that burn," into the very soul. *God is averse to sin,—he loves the pure and holy.* There must be in such an aversion, and in such a love a burning intensity corresponding to the ineffable greatness of the ideas, and the ineffable glory of Him of whom they are predicated. God is either wholly indifferent to what we call moral action, and then, of course, all moral ideas of every kind are but an empty delusion, or there is in the wide universe no wrath, as there is no love, that can be compared for intensity to that of Deity. They are measures of each other; as is the glowing heat, so is the melting tenderness; there is no love if there is no aversion, and this aversion is either an infinitesimal quantity, it is nothing at all, or it is all that Scripture includes, and more than we can conceive, in those fearful words, "*the wrath of God.*"

The abstract logical declaration may be given to the reason, and the reason may logically infer the infinity. Still it is a speculative infinity; the greatness, thus computed, is a mere mathematical greatness ; it is like the chemist's talk of caloric, or the optician's discourse of light. For divine truth, therefore, as distinguished from the natural and the speculative, there is needed that which "surpasses knowledge," even the strength and life of the spiritual emotion. Otherwise we philosophically resolve the wrath into a mere show of wrath, and that as a mere police providence for the prevention of evil which after all our naming is, on such a view, only physical evil, whilst we resolve the love into an intellectual approbation, which becomes as morally powerless as it is, in fact, philosophically unintelligible,—approbation of right having nothing by which it can be logically differenced from the approbation of mathematical or physical truth, and, in fact, the very idea of right running down into a mathematical conception of quantity, or calculation of physical pleasures and pains. If such a truth of Deity, then, is to be given to human minds at all, as a moral truth,—that is, as a power instead of a notion, as a life instead of a dead formula,—it must be through human language and imagery, as presented in the most vivid manner to human conceptions. In Divine truth, it must be kept in mind, it is depth, it is *intensity* we want, more than *comprehensiveness*, or mere completeness of logical statement. Hence the anthropomorphism and anthropopathism of the Bible. Hence the awful Hebrew figures, the חרון אף "the burning heat of this great wrath." And yet, what is called the bare abstract or ethical proposition, as expressed in terms purposely chosen, it may be, on account of their supposed mildness and abstractness, may be found to have a tremendous power, if we only carry our conceptions down to the roots of the words, or transfer the same image from a language where it has become trite—that is, worn and defaced—to another, where it comes out new and full of its old life. Thus the declaration: "*God is averse to sin*," might be chosen by some as being the milder mode of speech. It does not sound so harsh as when we say, "God hates." And yet, in truth, how fearful the figure of these mild words when transferred to Deity: the divine *aversion!* God's *turning away* his face! It is something he cannot look upon. There is no such turning away in nature; there is no such repulsion in all physical law. It reminds us of the language of Pindar when he speaks of the punishment of Tartarus.

τοὶ δ' ἀπροσόρατον οκχέοντι πόνον,[1]

or of Habakkuk's strong picture—"Thou art of purer eyes than to behold evil. Thou canst not *look upon* iniquity." Compare also Isaiah 3:8, "Their tongue and their doings are against the Lord, *to offend the eyes of his glory.*" How sharp and clear it there comes out, and yet it is the same image so worn, yea, almost obliterated, in what seems our

[1] Pindar Olymp. 2, stroph. 4: "A woe the eye cannot endure."

milder and more abstract phrase. It is this thought, too, that gives so much strength to the opposite figure as we so frequently find it in the earnest supplications of the Psalmist—

> "O, turn thee to my soul,"

and that ineffable image, or image of the ineffable, "Lift thou upon us, O Lord, *the light of Thy countenance:* O hide not Thy *face* from me ; put not Thy servant away in wrath ; Thou hast been my helper ; O leave me not, O cast me not away, thou God of my salvation." The ethical formula has been rendered cold and dead in the hands of the unfeeling logician, but when breathed upon by the Living Spirit, and thus recoined and stamped anew for the living soul, it has all the emotion of the most impassioned language, "*Ne avertas faciem tuam a me.*" "O turn not thou away." Thine *aversion* is death. "In thy favor is life ;" "in thy *presence* there is fulness of joy for ever more."

The reasoning employed applies not only to language expressive of the stern and fearful in the divine relations to us, but also to those moving expostulations that figuratively clothe themselves in the most tender of human images and emotions. What words shall express the love of God to his redeemed? "Can a woman forget her sucking child, that she should not have compassion on the son of her womb? Yea, she may forget, yet will not I forget thee, saith the Lord: I have graven thee on the palms of my hands; thy walls are ever before me." Is this the language of the Infinite? Does the Eternal Mind thus speak to us, not only through thoughts that necessarily run into the molds of the temporal and the finite, but in figures and images so purely, so intensely human? Yes, we answer, it is the language of the Infinite, when He converses with the finite. But are these His very words? Yes, His very words, chosen and arranged in every lineament and fibre of their Hebrew tenderness. Why not? Why stumble at surface objections when the whole difficulty lies far deeper. It is involved in the question: Can the Infinite reveal Himself at all in language in its widest sense of speech or outward sign, or in short, through any finite medium? Why talk of anthropopathism, as if there were some special absurdity covered by this sounding term, when any revelation conceivable must be anthropopathic. If made subjectively—as some claim it should be made if made at all—that is, to all men directly, through thoughts and feelings inwardly excited in each human soul without any use of language, still it must be anthropopathic. There is no escape from it. Whatever comes in this way to man must take the measure of man, and every essential objection now made would still have the same essential force. The thoughts and feelings thus aroused would still be human, and partake of the human finity and imperfection. In their highest state they will be but shadows of the infinite, figures of ineffable truths. Carry out the objection, then, and it is a denial of the possibility of any communication between God and man.

CHAPTER IV.

THE DENIAL OF THE SUPERNATURAL — This objection of Anthropopathism involves the Denial of the Supernatural — It allows of nothing aside from the One Total Movement of the Universe — The Human Soul demands the Supernatural — The Horror of Naturalism — Analogy between the Divine and the Human Supernatural — Credibility of the Reason as opposed to the Credibility of the Sense — The Objection to Miracles grounded solely on the Latter — The Real Wonder, Why does not God oftener speak to us? — The Supernatural in the Morning and Noon of the World — Will come again in the Evening — Has its place in the Great Chronology, or Order of the Ages.

BUT we cannot stop here. Such denial of all intercourse between the Infinite and the finite mind can only end in pantheism, or the perfect identification of God with the world. As there can be no special, so there can be no supernatural manifestation of any kind. There can be no action *in* nature, or *upon* nature, that is not *through* the whole, and so truly an action *of* the whole. There is no supernatural; there can be no supernatural. Now the man who asserts this, unless he intends the merest play of words, making every thing to be natural simply because it is some how in the universal system of things, has undertaken a defence of a position more *incredible*, that is, more opposed to the common judgments and feelings involved in the very laws of our thinking, than all the legends of all the revelations, real or supposed, that have ever claimed the credence of mankind. This argument of incredibility is commonly used against the miraculous, but it may be turned the other way, at least in one, and that its highest, aspect. The credibility of *sense*, we may admit, is much opposed to any special movement in nature, or to any interruption of its totality; the credibility of *reason*, if we may employ that term for some of the most interior as well as most catholic decisions of the soul, is powerfully in the other scale. There is something within us that demands the supernatural, that creates a disposition to believe in it, yea, an impassioned longing for it, even though that longing be so seldom sensibly gratified. It is as much a part of our spiritual constitution as the habitual belief in nature's regularity ; it is even a stronger and more interior acting of the soul, inasmuch as it has maintained itself, in all ages, against so much of adverse outward association. It is, in this respect, like the kindred belief in the soul's existence after death. In either case, there is something within us that holds us up, and carries us on, in spite of sense. The most visible of phenomena are against the one ; *common* experience opposes the other ; yet both hold on their way in the world, though miracles are few and far between, and fewer still come back from the unknown land. Generations pass away and are seen no more ; all things seem to continue as they were from any known beginning, and yet the disposition to believe, and the belief itself, are strong as ever. Instead of asking the aid of any inductive reasoning for its proof, it defies the power of any such reasoning, or of any reasoning, to drive it from the human soul. So also is there a "law in our minds" warring with the common experience of the slow unvaried movements of the physical world. We see the strength of it when science has laid bare evidence of what looks like some ancient break in nature's movements. It is one of the great charms of our modern geology. The naturalist, with all his fondness for talking of law and causation, cannot conceal the interest he takes in such discovery. He loves to find it so; it is not against his expectation when he does find it so. The pleasure he experiences reveals the law of his spirit, higher, deeper, and more unchanging than any law of nature. The discovery, we say, when made, is found to be just what might have been expected; it is in the highest degree rational, yea, truly credible; and even some who are most opposed to the Scriptural miraculous as bringing too near the idea of a personal God, do yet rejoice in a supernatural that is so ancient and so far off.

The thought of being ever buried in this shoreless, bottomless, sea of nature, of being as truly in it and parts of it whilst in our thinking, conscious state, as when our dead atoms are dispersed throughout its measureless abyss, is suffocating to the rational soul. It is a living death, and how any thinking mind can bear it, yea, even be fond of it, is the real marvel. Supernatural ourselves, as we consciously are, we may reasonably expect, and mankind have ever thus expected, to be conversed with, sometimes, in a supernatural manner. Constantly performing acts in opposition to, as well as in accordance with, the inward and surrounding nature, nothing is more natural, if we may use a seeming paradox, than that we should expect a similar display of power from the higher or superhuman plane. To our microscopic vision, it is, indeed, true, that the greater divine movements must necessarily appear immensely slow, or rather, with immense intervals between them as computed by our time measures, and as compared with our own rapid changings; but shall God ever be bound where we are free? "Is there in us," says Cicero, repeating the argument of Socrates, "Is there in us mind and reason, and shall there be mind nowhere else in the universe?" It is an argument for the existence of a God, but it is also an argument for the divine supernatural and its manifestations. *Necesse est Deum haec ipsa habere majora.* Is there in us a power of will, and do we exercise that power to control the physical forces around us, within certain limits, so that they do not produce the effects they would have produced without this uncaused spiritual intervention,—is there in us, we say, such a supernatural power, and shall it be nowhere else in the worlds above us—in God, or in higher superhuman beings acting as the ministers of God?

The analogy, it may be said, is not conclusive : it is but analogy, after all, and we cannot thus reason from the finite to the infinite. And yet, if it be true analogy, and not mere fancy, it must have a meaning. It is ἀνὰ λόγον, it is in *ratio*, or reason, with something higher, and we must infer from it that there is that in God which corresponds to this contra-natural or spiritual action in man. This reasoning from ourselves is no *sense* induction, like that which denies the credibility of the supernatural, or of a revelation to the finite, but is truly *a priori*, as grounded on ideas we find within us, or laws of thought out of which we cannot think. If the finite rational soul is an image of God, then such analogy, though falling immeasurably short, is, at least, in the true direction ; it is in the line of the absolute verity, and this is much, however remote the sighted object, or however reduced the scale on which the sighting index turns. The philosophic abstraction, on the other hand, commencing with the unknown infinite, may be a total aberration from the very beginning. In the other view, the compass points right, however distant the unseen pole to which it tends. It is like the mathematician's infinite series; we may not count their number, but we know the law of the final term. Hence may we rationally conclude, that God has given for our guidance this *analogy* or *proportion* of ideas; and if so, it must have this closing cadence, or else there is an abrupt and painful break, an unresolved dissonance in the harmony of thought. In a mere fanciful analogy, such dissonance is soon detected; but this is one of the most perfect kind, the more magnified, the more correct; it is without a deviation or a suspension as far as our reason traces it; it is, too, in most perfect accordance with Holy Writ, and with that language its author has chosen as most peculiarly and deeply human. Even if it is not conclusive, as they say,—even if we cannot follow it out to the point of logical necessity, that is, to that last ter n in the series where one idea is seen clearly lying within the other, still, as analogy merely, it accounts for the universal feeling, and this is all that is demanded for our present argument of credibility.

The supernatural is credible. It has its ground in that law of thought which is most catholic in our humanity, which is most inwardly removed from all surface differences; and hence it is so hard to understand men who seem to be of the opposite temperament, who believe that all is nature, and seem to be fond of so believing. The wonder, in fact, is not so much the occurrence of the supernatural as its rarity. Why is there not more of it? Why this painful reserve? All right, doubtless, so faith answers; for it requires faith sometimes, a divine faith we mean, to have a true belief in the natural as well as in the supernatural. But still the spirit asks, and may ask with reverence and humility, "Why standest thou afar off?" Why do not the heavens open? Why does not

God talk to us more frequently? Why does He not speak to us in our own human language, our own human thoughts and feelings, instead of those dull unchanging signals of nature that carry the general dispatches of the universe, (the physical universe with its exclusively physical intelligence) but have no news for us, no special word for us, no look of recognition for us, nothing, in short, to make us feel that we are either generically or individually before the Infinite Mind,—that God is thinking of us, not merely as present somewhere in His vast and total thought, but as a race remembered, as individuals known by name, known in our finity, known, in some sense, "even as we know."

If the vision tarry we wait long for it; we may never see it in our brief earthly stay, but we cannot surrender the thought. To believe that there never has been anything above nature, that there never will be anything *out of* nature, our souls, if we have souls, tell us is nothing but sheer atheism.

We may believe in "a God who hideth himself," but not in one who hideth himself forever. The Scriptures do, indeed, tell us that "God covereth himself with light as with a garment," but this is very different from being bound in an everlasting physical causation without interruption or suspension. This enrobing light is His supernatural glory, and finite eyes may see it, although they may never approach the direct vision of Him who dwelleth therein. But the thought of an endless nature is insupportable. Such an eternal future would seem to necessitate, in our thinking, a like eternal past of uninterrupted physical causation ; and then, where are we? Every argument for the existence of God is gone ; the very notion is gone. If, on the other hand, there have been beginnings and transitions in the past, then will there be again beginnings, and transitions, and interruptions, and suspensions in nature, in other words, displays of supernatural power. A little thinking shows us how much more rapidly the shadow must move, or seem to move, over the plain of our magnified earthly history, than on "the dial plate of eternity," and so we rationally make allowance, in our estimate, for the chronological rates in the vast divine epochs as compared with our swiftly passing days. The immensely enlarging lens of our microscopic *sense* is all filled with the vision of the natural, but our *reason* cannot give up the thought of the higher movement. We cannot surrender the idea, that in this greater chronology there are truly "years of the right hand of the Most High," great transition periods wherein "things do not continue in all respects as they were," but the scenes are shifted for the introduction of new acts in the drama of the ages. We cannot yield the thought of the supernatural, not only as having been in the days of our fathers when the world was new, but as expected still to be verified somehow, if not in our own individual experience, at least somewhere, and at some time, in the experience of the slow, long-living race. In the evening, as in the morning and noon of humanity, there will be the supernatural light. It must come again before the career of earth is run, or surely then, at that great *συντέλεια τοῦ αἰῶνος*, or "reckoning of the ages," when the natural, "which is first," shall be found to have been only a patient training, or a training of patience, for the higher spiritual experience. Is, then, the supernatural credible in any sense—that is, may the Infinite Mind and Power ever act out of the whole of nature, or manifest himself to the finite in any partial separate finite acts or forms, then is it credible that He may so manifest himself to the human soul, and thus converse with the human soul. Then is revelation credible, a revelation in language, a written revelation, a book revelation. If reason is not shocked at this, if reason demands it, though sense or the majority of experiences be against it, then is it also credible and rational, yea, demanded by this higher law of the spirit, that such revelation should be in the language that is the most human, in words, figures, and representative phenomena, most obvious, most primary, to the universal human race.

CHAPTER V.

THE OBJECTION MUST GO FARTHER — NO DIVINE KNOWLEDGE OF THE FINITE — God cannot know our Knowledge — We are known only in the Total Idea — The God of the Bible transcends this — He Thinks our Finite Thoughts as well as his own Eternal Thought — Feels Our Feelings — Knows our Consciousness — "In Him we Live, and Move, and Are" — The Scripture Pantheism — The False Pantheism — The real Danger, the Denial of the Divine Personality — The Seclusion of the Soul — God knows it by a knowledge, not A Posteriori from Effects, or A Priori from Causes, but Present and Ever Knowing — Does God know our Sin as we know it? — The Great Mystery — The Transcendental Objection itself Anthropopathic — Because We cannot ascend to God, therefore, it says, He cannot come down to us — The New Platonic Essence, above Knowing as above Being Known — The Scientific theism — Contrast of the Bible Language — Sublime Ascriptions of Personality.

BUT neither is there any stopping here. He who makes such denial of the anthropopathic, and hence of the supernatural, as being both of them impossible or irrational, must take another step. If God cannot so separate himself from nature as to make a revelation of the finite, and to the finite, then he cannot be truly said to *know* the finite as such. For thus to know, according to any conception we can have of it, and on which we can ground any assertion respecting it, is as much finite as the thinking or speaking connected with the *knowing* or the *making known* the knowledge. The Infinite intelligence becomes thus an intelligence only of infinity and totality. It cannot think the finite or the partial. They are utterly below it, and thus far away out of its sight, even as the infinite is above us. We are, therefore, unknown to God in any such way, either in degree or kind, as we are known to ourselves. So far, indeed, as the knowing, or mode of knowing, whether regarded as action or passion, is a part of the knowledge, it may be said we are utterly unknown to him. He has no *scientia* of our *conscientia ;* He does not know our consciousness ; for surely he cannot know *our* knowledge—*all* our knowledge—unless he know it, too, as we know it. He cannot think our thoughts as we think them ; and so it would follow that he cannot truly think them as they are. He cannot think our thoughts, as we cannot think his, and so it would follow, that as we cannot know the divine, so he cannot know the human as well as the divine. Now who shall dare assert this? "Who hath so known the mind of the Lord," that under the pretense of elevating, he should thus actually venture to limit the divine knowledge. Wherein, too, is this transcendental conception any better than the extra-mundane conceit of the sensual Epicurean? That is anthropopathic, it says; it is a representation of sensual ease yielding up to nature the care of the world. But may there not be a similar charge against the loftier view, as it would assume to be? With all its affected spirituality, it becomes itself only another form of this so much dreaded anthropopathism; it limits Deity in his relations to us by the same rule that limits us in our relations to him. We cannot rise to God, and therefore, it anthropopathically reasons, He cannot come down to us.

But the God of the Scriptures transcends any such *limiting* conception. "He inhabiteth eternity;" "He filleth all things." Philosophy may talk ever so proudly, she can never go beyond this. His unchangable abode is the infinity of time and space, and yet he thinks the finite truly, as finite, and as it is thought by the finite intelligence. This is the transcending mystery of the Bible; it presents both these wondrous aspects of Deity, and that, too, without betraying, on the part of the divine messengers, any feeling of dissonance, any misgiving sense of contradiction. God is so far off that all differences of space and rank vanish before him, and yet is he "nigh, very nigh to every soul that calleth upon him." "The Heaven and Heaven of Heavens cannot contain him, and yet he hath a house on earth where he records his name." "All nations are as nothing before him, yea, less than nothing and vanity," and yet he hath a people, a chosen people, a very peculiar people, whom he guides with a cloud by day and a pillar of fire by night. "He dwelleth in the high and holy place, yet hath he respect unto the contrite and the lowly." He hath given all things their law, and yet "he stoopeth down," in the minuteness of his providence, to behold every event that takes place in the heavens and in the earth. "He knows the end from the beginning." In that Eternal Mind lies ever undivided the total idea, the total movement, the total time of the immeasurable universe; "all things stand forever according to his unchanging ordinance;" "He maketh peace in his high places," and yet he hears continually the prayers of his elect. "He putteth their tears in his bottle," "He numbereth the hairs of their heads." Both views belong to the greatness as well as the harmony of the divine character,—great in its condescending depths, as in its ineffable height. God sees all things in their causes, he sees also all things in their effects and as effects, even as they are seen and known by us: He sees them in the infinite, total idea, He sees them also as parts, and in their ever varied, ever varying relations: He sees them as ever present, He sees them in their flowing successions; He sees them in their timeless being, before all worlds, He sees them as they are carried out in the utmost finity of their sense or phenomenal generation. He is the *'Ακίνητος*, the Immovable, whom Aristotle sought to comprehend—"*He changeth not,*" and yet, as the same philosopher attempts to describe him, so the Scriptures set him forth: He is the *ἀρχὴ ἧς ἡ οὐσία ἐνέργεια,*[1] the Eternal Principle, whose very essence is energy; "He speaks and it is done, He commands and it stands;" He is ever acting in all the changing appearances of nature; "He sendeth forth his commandment upon the earth; his Word runneth very swiftly."

The other view affects to be the philosophical one; it assumes to take the transcend-

[1] Aristot. Metaph. xi. (xii.) c. 6.

ing aspect of deity, excluding altogether the side that is turned to us, the finite side of the Infinite, as we need not fear to call it, or that in which God manifests himself to us as finite beings. It looks upon the Scriptural style as a mere accommodation to lower minds, and yet it is itself as deficient in grandeur as in moral power. Its deity is an abstract idol as false as any that was ever imagined or fashioned by the sense, as much removed from all sympathy and all communion as the veriest block that was ever worshipped in a heathen temple. But "our God is a great God and a great king above all Gods; in His hand lie all the deep places of the earth;" in that fathomless intelligence lie all the knowledges, and experiences, and even sentiencies of finite earthly souls. Why should we fear to take this ground. We call God the Infinite Reason, the all comprehending reason, why is He not also the all pervading Knowledge, the eternal Experience, the universal Sense? If we are made in the image of God, then must there be that in the Original, which, however transcending, corresponds to what is essential in the features and constitution of the spiritual copy. "In Him we *live*, and *move*, and have our *being*." If this be pantheism, it is the pantheism of the Scriptures, and we need not be afraid of it. There is another kind that has grown out of aversion to the deeply religious idea of the divine personality, and which would mimic the great truth whilst stripping it of all that would make it precious. But "our God is greater than the God" of the false pantheism, greater than the philosopher's transcendental deity. He is all-mighty, and can do all this that they, in the weakness of their human conception, deny to Him. He can have His infinite and, at the same time, his finite side, of being. He has his own eternal thought, and can also think, and does constantly think the thoughts of time. He is all knowing, and, therefore, more intimately present in our souls, yea spiritually nearer to us, we may say, than we are to ourselves.

Do we sufficiently think what is meant by the proposition, God knows us? It cannot be merely the knowledge of induction, that is, of causes from effects, however accurate and complete; it must be something more than the converse or complement of this, or the *a priori* knowledge of effects from causes. It cannot be perfect knowledge, an *all knowing* of all that we are, unless there be an ever present spiritual beholding, a constant actual knowing of our knowledge, and thinking of our thoughts. It is an idea most precious as well as fearful, and we may, therefore, dwell upon it for a moment, though leading to a seeming digression. Who is so unthinking as not to be sometimes impressed with that great mystery of our spiritual being, his own utter isolation from an all-surrounding universe? How perfect the seclusion in which every individual finite soul dwells apart from every other! We do, indeed, hold an imperfect intercourse by telegraphic signals passing through matter, but walls of adamant could not more effectually separate us from direct spiritual communing than the state in which God has created us. There is something impressively solemn in this deep seclusion, this everlasting loneliness. No other soul knows us; no other finite spiritual eye has ever seen us; the nearest friend has only inferred our existence; like the natural belief in a God, "our invisible things are understood from the things that are seen," even our inward power and humanity. The thought is sometimes our pride; it places in such gloomy grandeur each soul's inviolable individuality. It may also give rise to a feeling tinged with melancholy. O, could another know us, we are sometimes ready to exclaim, just as we know ourselves; we would be willing even that he should know our sins, could he also feel and know, to the fullest extent, all the palliations to which they are entitled in human eyes.

The most unthinking must have some experience of this. There are times when we are lonesome, insupportably lonesome, and then, is it fear, or joy, or are they both combined in the thought that there is, indeed, one who does thus know us. It may startle us when we think of all that is to be seen, and more, perhaps, than our own inner sense has ever seen, in that deep dwelling of our spirituality; truly is there pain, but this is not the only feeling; there may be consolation in the thought, yea even strength and joy. There is one Soul that knows us, personally, intimately, thoroughly,—knows us not by media, by signals outward or interior, not by induction from effects, or by foreknowledge from causes, but by direct and immediate presence, by more than presence, even by spirit-pervading, interpenetrating spirit,—not only an occasional or partial beholding, but an unintermitted knowledge of our *all*, our sense, our memory, our intelligence, our consciousness, even when least sensible, least known, least conscious to ourselves. "Thou hast possessed my reins; thou knowest my thought; when I awake I am still with thee." And then to think of this Soul thus pervading all other souls,—forming the universal medium, if we may use a term so much profaned, of all spiritual existences, and yet losing nothing of that distinct personality which it presents to each, nor impairing, in the least, that distinct individuality with which every finite spirit stands before the Infinite. There is in such a view, all that the highest philosophy can demand, and yet all that meets our lowliest human thought, our deepest human sympathy. There are indeed some startling questions here: How can God thus know us *thoroughly*, without knowing our sin, and how can he know our sin, *as it is*, unless he know it as we know it, that is with *con-scientia*, and how can he *thus* know it, and yet be sinless? since in our case we cannot conceive of the knowledge without the stain. It is like the other great mystery of the Redemption: How Christ can take our guilt and yet be guiltless? They are questions that must be left unsolved, and yet the great truth is one we cannot yield: God is of purer eyes than to behold evil, yet must he know it with a deep intelligence transcending that of any other mind in the universe. We inevitably fall into pantheism and a pantheistic impersonality, unless we hold fast to the truth, that there is no knowledge *of* the finite, and no knowing *by* the finite, that is not at the same time perfectly known, both as knowledge and knowing, as thought and thinking, to the Infinite One.

The transcendental objection, we say, does itself limit the divine perfection by allowing of no other aspect than that of the eternal and universal. It would pretend to magnify Deity by absorbing all things into the infinite. "But our God is the great God," from the very fact that he can thus withdraw, as we may say, within His infinity, while still remaining infinite. There is a distinction in the divine personality (so revelation teaches) by which he can do this, whether we can understand it or not. He can remain in his high, immovable, prime causation, whilst yet "the Divine Word," which is God himself, "runneth very swiftly" through all nature and all natural worlds. Yea, what seems a greater mystery, he can abide in his eternity, his immutability, his sublimity, and yet humble himself, and take the form of man, and the thought of man. He thus comes down to us in the written Word, so full of the divine majesty, the divine holiness, and yet so purely, so intensely human. He comes still nearer to us in the incarnate Word, "the Word that became flesh and dwelt among us;" and nearer still when Christ took upon himself our sins, and carried our sorrows, making himself our sacrifice, and thus becoming our "Great High Priest," who, even now, "in the highest heavens," can be touched with a fellow feeling of all our infirmities.

Ineffable is the mystery involved in all this, but the fact can be clearly stated, and reason must assent to the glory of the truth, even where it utterly fails to comprehend. We cannot ascend to Heaven, but God can come down to us ; we cannot become divine, but it is within his almighty power to become human, and thus lift us up to communion with himself whilst we still remain human. We can only take these thoughts as they are revealed to us in the Scripture. What, however, we cannot understand in its positive nature, may be distinctly and rationally summed up in its negative aspect. True it is, then, we say—and no transcendental thinker can go beyond the Bible thought in this—true it is, that "as the heavens are high above the earth, so is God's thinking above our thinking," and yet if he cannot *also* think our thoughts as we think them, feel our feelings as we feel them, know our knowledge as we know it, whilst, at the same time, dwelling evermore in his own high, unchangeable intelligence,—if God cannot do this, then are there "deep places" in his universe of soul unknown to him, unknown to him as they truly are; then his very infinity becomes his imperfection, his limitation, and there is really no divine knowledge of finite things according to any possible human thought of it. We have run up, or run down, to that hypernoetic essence of the later Platonists which makes the mind of God to be as much above all personal knowing, as all *being known.*

How far this blank nihility of thought in respect to the divine intelligence is from atheism, at least in any moral sense, it would be hardly worth our while to inquire. Infinity thus regarded is impersonality, and it is this and not the mere pantheistic idea that annihilates all religion. There is, as we have said, a Scripture pantheism; there is a true sense in which "God is all and in all;" there is a true sense in which it is said, "In him we live, and move, and are;" but this recognizes his personality and our personality as all the more distinct from the very fact of the inter-subsistence. "Because *He* lives *we* shall live also." Those little words *He* and *we* retain here all their measureless significance. "As Jehovah liveth, and as thy soul liveth :" In this remarkable Hebrew formula, the distinct personality and yet the inseparable interdependence is made the ground of appeal as the clearest and most immutable fact on which to establish the immutability of the oath. We may believe that "God is all," that God is the world, or the soul of the world ; we may or may not understand what we mean by this ; but if along with it we cleave, as for our very lives, to the truth that this great One and All, as we may call him, and scripturally call him, does truly think of us as finite beings, that we are truly present to that Eternal Mind, lying in it, embraced by it, but still as personalities, the finite images of the infinite personality, known as such, cared for as such, held accountable as such, treated, in fact, as spiritual persons and not as mere links in a physical system, or endless chain of things—if we cleave to this, then all that we need for morality and religion, or any religious hope, are preserved to us in all their saving integrity. "This God is our God, and we are his people, the flock of his pasture, and the sheep of his hand." We may send our thoughts to any extent in the one direction, if we never lose that hold of prayer and conscience that binds us to the other. We may indulge in any views of the divine infinity, of the universal life, of the one universal, all-embracing thought, and yet feel that our almost infinitesimal finity is as distinctly recognized as though it had been alone with God, the only act and object of his creating power. Such is the language of faith transcending all calculations of quantity and extent. "Fear not, only believe." There is no vastness in which we can be lost. "Fear not, thou worm Jacob, I have redeemed thee, saith the Lord, I hold thee by thy hand, I have called thee by thy name; thou art mine." "Why sayest thou, O Israel, my way is hid from the Lord, and my judgment is passed over from my God? Hast thou not known? Hast thou not heard that the Everlasting God, the God of eternity, Jehovah, the Creator of the ends of the earth, fainteth not, neither is weary? There is no searching of his understanding. He giveth power to the faint, and to them that have no might he increaseth strength. Even the youths shall faint and be weary, and the young men shall utterly fall; but they that wait upon the Lord shall renew their strength; they shall mount up with wings as eagles; they shall run and not be weary, they shall walk and not faint."

There may be also a scientific theism which is no better than pantheism, and may be even less religious. It is less philosophical, too, and steers clear of pantheism only at the expense of reason and consistency. It shuts God out of nature, out of the world, puts in His place the idol law, all the while assigning to deity, with the utmost show of deference, some extramundane, overlooking, sphere, whence he never interferes with nature's everlasting work. Such theism, we say, has even less of a religious ground than the false pantheism. The one so absorbs the world in God as to destroy all idea of the divine personality; the other seems to preserve the distinction and the personality, but renders it of no account by severing it wholly from the natural and the human, except as a mere name for the remote unknown originating power. Both are children of the same parent. Both are vulgar though affecting great profundity. Pantheism may be revived by modern schools, as something wonderfully transcending ordinary conceptions, but it is very early and very common. It has existed, exists now, where there is the least of culture and truly educated thought. The Buddhist priests of Thibet or Siam are far beyond, in this respect, the philosophers of Boston or of Westminster. The untaught plodder in the secluded mechanic's shop has thought out all this philosophy for himself, and been surprised to find that it was so well known before. So also naturalism has flourished, and flourishes still, with the crudest science. Lucretius and the Epicureans could talk of law—*ἀρχαὶ*, *principia*, *principles*, they called it—as profoundly as any modern savan. The lecturers on phrenology indulge in the same lingo with as much confidence as the most scientific astronomer or geologist. And they have the same right to do so. Both classes of ideas, whether they assume the pantheistic or the naturalistic form, are products of the common thinking as affected by the common depravity. Both have something of reason in their paternity, but their common mother is an evil conscience. They are born of the moral dislike, the moral dread of the idea of a personal deity. They are both but the unrest of souls that in their flight from this personal God would find some halting short of that lowest abyss of a dark, idealess, wholly unintellectual atheism.

On either view, this idea of the divine personality is lost. That which cannot recognize the finite, whether *in itself*, or out of itself, or below itself, can have itself no self-hood; since it can have nothing of which it can think (aside from the total idea) much less any thing to which it can speak, or by which it can properly be invoked. Personality implies relation, mutuality, plurality, or duality at least. As predicated of deity it involves either the eternity of the world, as some of the ancient minds held on this very ground, or else eternal personal distinctions in the divine being, the idea to which other ancient minds resorted to solve the awful difficulty. Deity could not be thought except as having itself its eternal *thought*, its eternal *love;* and hence that very old idea of the divine Paternity, with its *Νοῦς* and *Ψυχὴ*, which Pythagoras and Plato are said to have brought from the East. Or did it not rather come from revelation, from the going forth in the world of that early language we find in the very beginning of Genesis, and which the neological interpretation can never satisfy,—the Word and the Spirit in creation, and that mysterious allocution at the birth of humanity, "Let *us* make man in *our* image." It is, however, enough for our present argument to hold the thought in reference to created personalities. Whatever we may think, or fail to think of the divine pre-existence, still, as regards any personal conceptions we can form of deity, the *ego* is inseparable from the *tu* and the *ille*. In other words, there can be no first person *in* him *to* whom there is no second, and *of* whom, and *by* whom, there is no third. When, in such a statement, we are compelled to use the words *in him*, we have already the language of personality, thereby implying the inherent logical contradiction in the contrary supposition, or its utter repugnance to the God-given laws of human thought. We cannot think at all, much less speak, of God; he cannot use the *ego* or speak *to* us in any way, or tell us of *himself*.

Any language implying such a self-hood becomes as much anthropopathic as any ascriptions to deity of human affections, or human bodily actions, or bodily organs. Though not in the same degree, perhaps, yet as truly and as essentially does it present the finite, and even the human aspect. "*Thou* art from everlasting unto everlasting"—"*He* dwelleth in light unapproachable and full of glory"—"*I* am the first and the last, saith the Lord, who is, and was, and is to come" —"Before the day was, *I* am *He*"—"And now, Father, glorify *thou me* with the glory that *I* had with *thee* before the world was." These certainly are transcending revelations; if human speech can convey any thought of God, it is here carried to its utmost height of grandeur, as well as lucidity; and yet all this glorious language is liable to the same objection of the man who denies the possibility of a finite written or spoken revelation. It is anthropopathic; it implies personality, and personal relations. It is the finite self-hood invoking the Infinite ; it is one eternal personality addressing another ; it is the Infinite speaking of *himself.* אהיה אשר אהיה, *ego sum qui sum, I am that I am,*—this sublimest declaration of human speech falls in the same category with what might seem the most extravagant figures of the Hebrew prophets.

CHAPTER VI.

IF REVELATION IS HUMAN, IT MUST BE MOST HUMAN — The Scriptures Written in the Heart of the Church — In the History of the World — The Scriptures have a Typical Significance — Typical Men, Viri Portendentes — Typical Facts — The Formula — "*Thus saith the Lord*"— Truly the Lord's Words — Yet Psychologically the Prophet's Words — In respect to Deity, One Finite Mode is as outward as another — Nature a General Epistle — Has no Intelligence for us, as Individuals, or a Race — Addressed to the Impersonal Scientific Reason — The Scriptures a Special Epistle, having *our* name, and Address to Humanity — The Media Specially Chosen — Excellency of the Scripture Language — Should be Used as much as Possible in Devotion — "Let us take with us Words and return unto the Lord."

LET us see clearly where we are. It is for this purpose we have dwelt so long upon this objection of anthropopathism. Carry it out, and God could not make a revelation in language, in *any* language, in any actions, signals, symbols, in any outward representations, in any inward affections of the soul, in any finite way, in short, that is either actually or conceivably separated from the one total action, the one indivisible and everlasting movement of the universe. If, however, the Infinite can make a revelation *to* the finite, and *through* the finite, then do these minor difficulties all vanish. If God can come down to us at all, then, with all reverence be it said, can we see a reason why, since all human language is radically underlaid, and must be underlaid, by images of sense, he should adopt, at once, that style of speech which is the most outward, the most phenomenal, and, therefore, the most universal. It is a typifying process. The media are the souls, the emotions, the thoughts, the imaginations of inspired men, but so chosen, so placed in form, and so worked, that the last outward impression should present that deep, sharp, well-defined letter, that may be clearly seen and read of all men. Revelation is the chapter of the supernatural, as given to us through inspired human agents. Along with this history of the supernatural, and through it, as a medium, it is also the vision of the divine ideas as they appear in human forms; and thus has it been engraven, stereotyped, we might say, indelible and imperishable, in the whole history of the world, even as God commanded the prophet—" Write the vision, and *cut it deep* on tablets, that he may run who readeth it."

But the Bible is not mere ink and parchment. It has been written on the heart of the Church, and thus has been, from age to age, the *living* as well as the *uttered* word. It has been deeply printed in the secular annals of the world; other histories being, in this respect, but its marginal scholia. It has carried with it, too, a typical significance, a sense, not new, but ever enlarging, that has made it, at every period, the law of the world's cycles, the only light that gives any meaning to its past, or can be trusted for any interpretation of its future. The events of Scripture are themselves *words* having a significance to be interpreted. They are representative events. The men of Scripture are representative men. They are אַנְשֵׁי מוֹפֵת, as was said of Joshua the High Priest, "men of type," or typical men, *viri portendentes*, ἄνδρες τερατοσκόποι,—συμβολικοί. They are *homines in signum positi futurorum*, as Hieronymus following his Jewish teacher admirably interprets Zach. 3 : 8. Thus regarded, the Scriptural histories are, at the same time, *fact* and *figure*. In respect both to men and events, they are typical histories—*res futuras res adumbrantes*. They are the forecast shadows of other cycles in the life of the world and the Church. Israel is the "chosen servant" to be "light to the Gentiles, and God's salvation, even to the ends of the earth." And thus the whole revelation, Jewish and Christian, is a *living* word, uttered continually in the great historical movement, and so connected with it, that take away this chapter of the supernatural and the supernatural people, and the key to all history is lost.

"Thus saith the Lord." They are truly the Lord's words. It is the veritable language of the Infinite speaking through media to the finite mind, even as one unseen human soul speaks to another human soul, through the outward undulations of the air. And yet we do not mar the thought of the infinite by any such conception. All things, in their imageless ideas, lie in that ineffable mind. But when God puts them forth in the forms of time and space, that is, *actually* thinks them and *utters* them, then one mode is as outward,—that is, to Deity, as finite, as much necessitated to some form of sense, or sense conception, or sense imagery, as another. Thus nature, too, as well as the Bible and history, is a language, though having a general message. It is a species of telegraphic, or far writing, conveying intelligence, but not *to* the individual soul as such, nor *for* the individual soul. It brings no intimation that such soul is present to the divine *thinking*, or has any special relation to the Infinite, or is at all known to Him except as indivisibly comprehended in the one total indivisible thought. The signals of nature are addressed to the impersonal scientific reason. Yet even thus viewed as a general language it has its difficulties of *expression* which no natural theology can decypher ; it has archaisms, or obsolete forms, of which we can give no reason in any present order of things ; it has apparent solecisms that we cannot reduce to syntax by any exegetical strain we may put upon them ; they look harshly, they sound barbarously, in spite of all our attempts to bring them into harmony with other moral, or even physical utterances. Our *a priori* philosophy would say they could not be divine,—that is, could not exist in the works of a perfectly wise and good and powerful being, if stubborn facts did not furnish the constant refutation. Nature is a general epistle, but the written revelation is purely human ; it is addressed to our race, and to each individual soul that reads or hears it. It has our name in the beginning and throughout. It is directed to humanity, and is, therefore, most human in its form. It is God's chosen language to us,—the words and images specially selected and specially arranged with a reference to the wants of our human race in their peculiar moral history. The media employed are all determined with respect to this. The age, the nation, the man, the mind, are all chosen to bring it out, and give it this utmost power of its representative fulness. "Thus saith the Lord,"—it is not a mere prophetic formula, expressive of a general thought or feeling, and leaving the filling up wholly to the human imagination of the Seer. We are not to believe this any more than the other or mechanical theory, which would represent the words as outwardly spoken to the Prophet's ear, or telegraphically signalled to his imaging sensorium. They are, psychologically, the Prophet's words, the Prophet's images, yet still none the less specially designed through the linked media of revelation, and thus divinely enunciated, as the very best possible words, the best possible imagery, through which such an approximate communication of the ineffable could be made to human minds. It is God's choice or chosen language to us ; and it should be, therefore, of all others, that which we should employ when "*we take with us words* and return unto the Lord." As far as possible, our prayers, our praises, our confessions, our thanksgivings, all our devotional intercourse with Deity should be in the very language of Scripture, —in that sacred speech which He has prepared and given to us, even as he originally taught to Adam the language of the common life and common wants. So shall we most worthily render "unto God the *fruit of our lips ;*" so "shall the words of our mouth and the meditations of our hearts be acceptable unto him who is our strength and our Redeemer." The hypocrite may pervert this Bible language, the fanatic may make it odious, worldly satirists may caricature it, clerical wits like Sidney Smith may ridicule it as puritanical cant; yet still to Christians must it continue to be the sacred dialect, God's chosen speech for his chosen people. They will not profane it by thoughtless use or secular parodies, yet still will they cling to it as the cherished vernacular of their new citizenship. In its wondrous depth, its celestial clearness, its critical edge,([2]) its "soul and spirit dividing energy," its thought-piercing, heart-revealing power, above all, in its awing impress of superhuman authority whilst yet speaking in such intensely human tones, they find it just the medium their souls want, and God has provided, for religious *thinking* as well as religious *utterance*,—the surest source, in short, of right feeling, right conception, and right speaking in all that relates to the spiritual and the divine.

CHAPTER VII.

Is the Bible Language Obsolete? — "Christ apprehending us" — God Laying hold of us in his Word — Accommodations — Apologies for the Bible Language — Have We advanced beyond it? — Holiness the true test of Progress in the Divine Ideas — A Progress in Revelation, but not for the Reason usually given — The Bible Language nearest to the Ineffable — The Philosophic style might have been employed—The Materials for it were very anciently in the World — Paul could have talked Platonically — The Old Testament Language produced a higher order of thought than that of any Eastern or Western Philosophy — Difference between the Jewish Outward and the Heathen Outward — Are the Modern Transcendentalists remarkably Holy Men? — Our Literary World — Our Political Men—Are they really more spiritual than Cicero or Tacitus? — Universality of the Scriptures.

God be thanked for the anthropopathism of the Scriptures. It is but another name for *human sympathy*. It is but another form of that same love which moved Christ to "take upon himself our nature," (if we adopt the old Patristic rendering of Heb. 2:16) or "to lay hold of us," to *apprehend us*, (according to the more modern exegesis,) when we were sinking, like Peter, in the overwhelming waters. He thus lays hold of us in his word that we may *think* of him as he thinks of us, that we may *know* him even as he knows us, "that we may *apprehend* that *in* which, or *through* which, we are apprehended of Christ Jesus." ([3]) We may affect to be above this condescension, to have grown out of it in the advance of the world, to have reached, in short, some spiritual eminence. where, for ourselves at least, we may dispense with it, and adopt a more philosophical style of thought and speech. Hence so much of what may be called apology for the Bible,—*apologies* strictly in the degenerate sense of the word,—excuses for the Bible, in fact, as being adapted in its dress and diction to a past age, though still possessing thought that may be better recast or recoined in the modern "Philosophies of Religion," or of Christianity, as they are styled. But this idea of obsoletism, though beginning to manifest itself in the more evangelical interpretation, as it assumes to be, is as false as it is irreverent. We would say also, as unphilosophical, were it not too much in the style of the very cant we are condemning. What is there in the spiritual condition of man in this nineteenth century of human darkness and depravity? What is there in any purer holiness, or any higher moral elevation we may fancy ours,—how much nearer, in this respect, do we stand to the ineffable truth, that we should claim to be addressed in a different style from that which was adapted to Patriarchs and Apostles, as though, through our advance in other knowledge, we had really reached a more spiritual or more holy state. For this, and not mere intellectuality, must be the true test. It is holiness, rather than knowledge, that makes us like God. It is love, humility, reverence, purity of heart that brings an individual or an age nearer to that which is most divine, most central, in the divine thought. Here is the real progress through which we make a real approach unto Deity ; this is the only progress that makes us better able to understand God when he speaks to us, whether it be in nature, in history, or in the Word. "The pure in heart shall see God." "Thou through thy commandments hast made us wiser than our enemies. I have more understanding than all my teachers, for thy testimonies are my meditation. I understand more than the ancients because I keep thy precepts."

Are we more holy, more loving, more unselfish, more obedient, more believing, than men of the olden time,—then, and just in that proportion of our higher holiness, and our more loving obedience, and our purer self-renouncing faith, may we hope that we are wiser in the divine ideas. Now who shall abide this test ? Will it be the men who have most to say in their writings, and in their lectures, of the obsoleteness of the Scriptures ? Are they the heavenly minded ones? Or will it be their admiring followers who regard them as the infallible oracles of the age? Will it be our literary classes generally who talk so much of refinement and culture? Have they this higher spirituality, this purity of soul that renders men Godlike and more capable of understanding God? To say nothing now of the vulgar or "dogmatic piety" as they would style it, are they really more distinguished than other men, or the men of other ages, for their unearthliness, their contemplation of the higher life, or that divine communion which even reason would tell us, must be the truest source of the truest divine knowledge? Are they, in all these respects, wiser, as they are more holy, than "the ancients?" Until convinced of this, we must continue to believe that Moses, and David, and Isaiah, stood nearer the divine thoughts than Strauss or Hegel,—that Paul and John were certainly as capable, to say the least, of receiving spiritual ideas, and a true divine knowledge as any of the men who are now known as the transcendental thinkers and lecturers of the times.

There is doubtless a progress in revelation; for the fact is announced in revelation itself. "God, who in times past spake unto our fathers by the Prophets, hath in these last days spoken unto us by His Son." But the reason of this must be sought elsewhere, if sought at all, than in any spiritual progress of man that may be supposed to keep in advance of it, or to be independent of it, or to have prepared men for it. Higher truths were revealed through Paul than were given to Joshua or to Samuel; but no reason can be assigned—none derived from history or any known condition of man—why the earth-wearied, heaven-seeking Patriarchs, why the thoughtful Arabian of the days of Job, why the Schools of the Prophets in the times of the seraphic Isaiah, might not have received into their souls the same spiritual truths that were afterwards received by the dark, dissolute, and brutalized inhabitants of Asia Minor. No reason can be given why the fuller revelation of God might not have been understood by these earlier men, these lofty, primitive minds, as well as it was afterwards received and understood by the savage Numidian, or the still fiercer Goth, or as it is now received by the worldly, the sensual, the ignorant, the unspiritual, of this nineteenth century. No reasons, we say, for this evidently designed progress in revelation, can be derived from history simply, or from any earlier or later culture of man as made known in history. They must be sought in revelation itself, or foregone as among the inscrutable mysteries of the divine government.

It is enough for us that revelation has not been dependent on human progress outside of it, and, therefore, its language cannot be rendered obsolete by it. The thought holds true, even if we take into the account the progress, or true spiritual culture, made through revelation itself. Those who have shared most largely in this spiritual culture, who have drank deepest at the fountain of Scriptural truth, are the last to wish any change, or to feel the need of any change in the divine communications. They are thankful for every type, for every metaphor, for every impassioned appeal, for every instance of the divine condescension in coming down to us, taking the scale of our thoughts, and speaking to us in our own human emotions, our own human conceptions, as well as in our own human words. They know as well as others,—they know better than others, that "God's thoughts are above our thoughts," and his thinking above our thinking, "even as the Heavens are high above the earth," but they also believe that in this Bible language there is the nearest earthly approximation to the ineffable truth, that the eye most intently fixed upon it—though at a vast distance, it may be—is yet in the true *direction* of the heavenly vision, and that the heart that loves it most is most directly, and most speedily, growing up into the fulness and reality of the heavenly life. Any substitution of a more philosophical or scientific dialect would be, thus far, a divergency from the true celestial line, from the straight course of the upward calling. It would fall short *in distance* as much as the other,—for in this respect all human intellects must be on a par—whilst, in regard to the first and far more essential idea, it would be *a total* failure, even inasmuch as an error in direction involves every other error. It would be, moreover, essentially false in proportion as it was destitute of that emotional power which makes the Scriptures the Living Word, the *truth alive* and vitalizing in the soul. If we may venture to carry the thoughts onward to a period in eternity when the ineffable truth contained in Christianity shall come directly before the spiritual vision, and be "seen face to face," then may it be found that they in this life were looking most directly in this line of *absolute verity* who kept themselves most docilely and submissively to the gracious "accommodations" of the Scriptures, not seeking to be above them, or to dispense with them, on any view, however outwardly respectful, of their being wholly or partially designed for a former more worldly or less spiritual age.

It is the Bible language in which the religious emotion ordinarily finds its most fitting vent. There are, it is true, ecstatic conditions, such as appeared in the miraculous powers of the early Church, in which the soul breaks out in an unknown tongue that has no interpretation in any earthly thoughts and images; and yet we have intimations that even in the higher world, the dialect of the early religious life is not wholly lost. John, indeed, saw the heavenly ideas through earthly eyes; the mysterious "living creatures" around the throne, the golden city, and the waters of life, may represent what is ineffable to us in our present thinking, yet still there are figures of the Sacred Writings, if we may call them figures, that even eternity will never efface from the soul's long memory. The Cross, the Crown, "the Lamb slain from the foundation of the world,"—these will be still the representatives of imperishable ideas. They will remain, still a language, in eternity as in time,—still a language, even when science shall be seen to have been only a reflection from a darkened mirror, and philosophy a childish talking, a childish thinking, long since put away among far off earthly things.

The philosophical style of speech could have been employed in the Scriptures, had their divine author regarded it as the best mode through which divine ideas could be conveyed to men. It not only existed in the world at a time when much of the older Scripture was written, but had reached a high degree of culture. The old Egyptian Mystics, the Eastern Pantheists, the early Ionian and Eleatic schools of the West, Xenophanes and Heraclitus the ancient

Hegel and Spinoza, were talking of ἀρχαὶ and ἄιτια, of *principles* and *causations*, of the "universal reason," the ὄντα and γιγνόμενα, the "being and the becoming," the objective and the subjective, the *me* and the *not me*, the One in all and the all in One, the everlasting flux and the eternal immobility,—all this not far from the time when Isaiah was setting forth in his burning figures the ineffable majesty of the Living God, before whom "the Seraphim veiled their faces with their wings, crying Holy, Holy, Holy, Lord of Hosts, the whole earth is full of his glory." The language of the Schools had been brought to its highest perfection (a perfection we think not even now surpassed) when Paul preached those stumbling-blocks to the world's religion and the world's philosophy,—the doctrines of the Cross and of the Resurrection. Is it said, then, that these were only apparent teachings of the Apostle, that they were defective forms of truth, mere accommodations in fact, because he had no higher language for the spiritual life and the divine favor than these gross Jewish anthropopathisms,—the only answer needed is a distinct denial both of the fact and the argument. Paul could have used the dialect of the wranglers in the famous gymnasia of Tarsus, he could have talked as spiritually as the Platonists, or as logically as the Aristotelians, or as mystically as the school of Philo, had he seen fit to do so; and in saying this, we need not make for him, as has sometimes been done, any extravagant claims in respect to learning; for the age was swarming with these disputants, and their public discussions and lectures, if not their books, were among the common phenomena of the times. He could easily have used their speech, and he would have been understood too, as well as philosophic language, so called, is understood by the masses at the present day; for all through the chief towns of the Roman Empire, at least where the Greek language was spoken, a smattering of this kind of talk had got down into the common mind, even as it has now filtered through the modern reading and lecture hearing world. The scoffer Lucian affords sufficient evidence, if we had no other, that Paul, had he chosen to talk philosophically, would have been as well understood at Athens, or Corinth, as Mr. Parker or any of his associates in Boston or New York.

There is an egregious fallacy here, whether we think of the later or the more ancient revelation. A fact may be appealed to as a conclusive refutation of all abstract reasoning on the subject; and this is, that the anthropopathism of the Old Testament, with its typical representations, *did* actually produce a higher order of thinking than the abstract style of any Eastern or Western philosophy. The ancient Jew, with his tabernacle made in all respects "after the pattern shown to Moses on the Mount," the cosmical (4) sanctuary or *world temple* typical of things in the Heavens," * with its lights and incense, the

* Heb. 9 : 11.

altar with its sacrifice, that sacrifice of which the heathen world had lost the meaning and for which its philosophy had no idea, the Ark of the Covenant, the Mercy Seat, the Cherubim with their overshadowing wings looking down upon its mystery, the Shekinah, the unapproachable Holy of Holies,—the ancient Jew, we say, through the ideas thus represented, knew more of God, of his adorable unity, his awful holiness, his intense hatred of sin and impurity, than was ever dreamed of in the "numerical ratios" of Pythagoras, or the "eternal ideas" of Plato; he had a more *living* thought of God's near personality, and, at the same time, his far-off inconceivable immensity, of his burning presence as their own patrial Deity, and, at the same time, his high unrepresentable glory transcending all similitude,* than ever came from all the speculations of the Academy or the Porch.

Some would compare these Jewish sym-

* Deut. 4 : 15.

bols with the outward in the heathen worship,—but the difference is immense; it is radical, and exclusive of all comparison. They were symbols of holiness, the others of impurity; they were symbols of the ineffable, the others of all that was most sensual in an outward and sensual mythology; they were symbols of the heavenly, as transcending nature, the others had almost wholly a physical idea. The Jewish rites had a spiritual power, although maintaining a holy reserve as to a spiritual world; the other had its fantastic supernatural, its wild demonology, and yet the whole tendency was to the earthly, the human, the lower than the human; for the prime consistency of these chaotic myths, and of this chaotic worship, was only found in making gods and daimones, as well as men and animals, all the children of one common mother nature. Hence there was really so much less religion among the heathen, even where they seemed to be more religious than the Jews. The former had no check upon their depraved imaginations; the chosen people had a stern ritual out of which the fancy was forbidden to wander. Hence, too, what has caused some to wonder, that the Greeks should have had what seemed a larger and more definite creed respecting Hades, and souls in Hades, than the Children of the Promise; and yet, to the thinking mind, how much more of moral impressiveness in the few hints of the Old Testament on this dread subject, its cautious speaking, its awful reserve, we may say, than in all the Greek fancies of Tartarus and Elysium. The future life was not concealed; there was a *hope* if not a distinct idea, a faith, purer perhaps from its very indefiniteness, that in some way, the dead, the righteous dead, at least, did still "live unto God," but the fulness and clearness of this revelation was reserved for the Conqueror of Hades. Such a doctrine was too precious to be given fully to the world before "the Interpreter" came, or to be prematurely submitted to the peril of mythical additions and deformities even among the chosen people. It was, therefore, for ages to have the form of pure trust in God, unaided, as it was unweakened, by any pictures of the fancy or any necrological view that might take the form either of poetry or philosophy. In the descent to the Greek Hades there was no such leaning on the divine arm, no such confidence as that in the strength of which the Psalmist ventured down into the *terra umbrarum*, or valley of the shadow of death; there was no faith like that which led the religious Jew, in view not only of the unknown but *unimagined* futurity, to exclaim, "Into thy hands do I commit my spirit; Thou hast redeemed me, Lord God of truth." For the Hebrew mind, the first great idea was God, his sovereignty and holiness, whatever might be the destiny of men; and this brings us back to the peculiar character of the Old Testament rites and symbols as compared with all others then in the world.

They were *holy*. They ever denoted the pure, whether in the soul itself or in the body, as typical of the spiritual cleanliness. They denoted *separation*, election, or setting apart for God. In a word, they were types of holiness, and in this they were as far removed from all heathen worship on the one hand, as from all heathen philosophizing on the other.

How small the intervals both of time and space, between the Hebrew prophets and the Greek philosophers! How preposterous, then, the notion that God chose the language of the former because the world had not yet made sufficient spiritual progress to be addressed in the more logical or intellectual style of the latter! How still more absurd is it when we are told that this Jewish mind, as represented by Paul, could not understand the more spiritual Greek as set forth in the school of Plato, or the high morality of the Stoics. With such a taste, for we can give it no higher name, it is impossible to dispute.

If any cannot see, or rather feel, how immeasurably the ethical ideas of the Apostles, to say nothing of the direct teachings of Christ, transcend those of Epictetus and Seneca, then all argument is thrown away ; the difference is radical and irreconcilable.

The absurdity, however, is more evident, it becomes even superlative, when it is assumed that the modern mind,—the common modern mind, we mean, as it appears in the ordinary literary and political life,—so far transcends in ethical purity both the Greek and Jewish ideas of the holy and the divine, that we need a new theological language, or that the old Scriptural style, though yet respected as the vehicle of ancient thought now obsolete, should be henceforth regarded as the "accommodating" teacher of those advanced conceptions of God and his eternal kingdom that have come from our modern æsthetics and our modern knowledge. In this view, so condescending whilst so conservative, the Bible is still to be retained like some rough though high-priced picture of the "old masters;" its antique setting even is to be undisturbed, and its strange coloring left untouched through regard for its venerable antiquity; but then it is to be associated with ideas of a higher order, and with such a "philosophy of religion" as probably the old writers would have taught had they shared in the present spiritual advance.

Now, to do justice to this modern claim, it must be treated according to the assumption it necessarily involves if it be a real progress, that is, a real spiritual progress. To be consistent with that undeniable test that has just been laid down, its chief ground of confidence can be rationally nothing else than some astonishing increase in holiness, unearthliness, and heavenly-mindedness, supposed to have been lately made in certain schools in Germany, and among those who speak of themselves as the leading thinkers of our own land. So clear as well as profound have been their discoveries of God and eternal things that an entirely new aspect has been given to theology. It is also to be maintained on the ground of a similar *general* advance in holiness, brought about through the influence of these "leading minds." Society in its common thinking is so much nearer heaven, nearer the empyrean of truth,—the literary world is so much more pure, the "educated classes," as they are called, are becoming so much less earthly, so much more occupied with divine contemplations, that we have a right to expect a higher style of revelation than was vouchsafed to former times. Some of the language we have just employed may seem strange as thus applied. This talk of superior holiness may strike even the supposed claimants as being somehow out of place, or as suggesting, in their case, inharmonious ideas. But surely this arrogant assumption of a spiritual advance carrying men beyond the spirituality of the Bible, means just this, means all this, or it means nothing.

Judged, then, by this standard, tried by

this test, what, we may ask in all seriousness, is our political world, our literary world, our "thinking class," our men of culture, that they should make this claim, or be supposed to occupy so much higher a position in respect to the unearthly things, or those great matters of eternity that have agitated the minds of men from the foundation of the world or the day when humanity first began to think or feel. What is there in the modern public man that places him, in this respect, above the public man of former times? To go no farther back into the remote past, wherein has he any advantage, except what the Bible gives him, if it gives him any, over the Roman senator? We say, if it gives him any, for unless it has had a direct converting, sanctifying, enlightening influence upon his soul, we may even regard the heathen as the nobler man. Christianity, if it has not raised, has lowered the other. The mere nominal profession, with its habitual and demeaning hollowness, has taken from the native manhood which appears so splendid in some of the historical examples of the olden time, whilst it has conferred no compensating heavenly grace. But select the highest modern specimens of this class. Wherein, we may well ask, does such a one show more spirituality than Cicero, a better hope than Agricola, a higher sense of the world's great evil than Tacitus? In short, take away the direct effects of regenerating grace on individual souls—for these are yet, as in the early centuries, the rare exceptions—and where is the great spiritual difference between our nominally Christian and the ancient heathen State?

It is, indeed, a most preposterous claim that is thus put forth on behalf of our social and literary condition, — especially as it is sometimes partially sanctioned in our modern preaching. We are not more unworldly than the Patriarchs, more spiritual than the Prophets, more heavenly-minded than the Apostles; we are not nearer the great celestial verities than men of the olden time, at least by any philosophy, or science, or culture of our own that is independent of the study and the grace of the Scriptures ; we are not beyond the Bible either in its letter or its thought. There are ideas there the world has not yet fathomed ; there are words and figures there whose rich significance interpretation has not yet exhausted. The Scriptural style and the Scriptural language are not meant for one age, but for all ages. Its orientalisms will grow in the west ; its archaisms will be found still young in the nineteenth century. Science is ever changing as it is ever unfinished, its language is ever becoming obsolete as it is ever superseded, philosophy is continually presenting some new phase of its ever-revolving cycles, the political world is ever a dissolving view, literature becomes effete and art decays, "but the Word of our God shall stand forever." Not so sure are the types of nature as even the form and feature of this written word, if it be indeed the *word of God*, uttered in humanity, breathed into human souls, informing human emotions, conceived in human thoughts, made outward in human images, and indissolubly bound, as the wondrous narrative of the supernatural, in the long chain of human history.

CHAPTER VIII.

THE ENDURING WORD—Christ's Declaration, Matt. v. 18—"Not one Iota shall fail"—The Reference is to the Spiritual Effect—Every Part of the Scriptures contributes to the Great Consummation—The True Textus Receptus—Written in the Heart of the Church Militant and Triumphant—The Living Word, the Living People—The Everlasting Codex—The "Fight of Faith"—The Bible Question ever calling out a New Power—The Problem it presents in History—No Human Intellect Competent to Solve it—Except on the Ground of the Supernatural—Other Sacred Books belong to but One Age—Are addressed to but One Phase of Humanity—Strange Universality of the Bible—The Rationalist has no Eyes for the great Wonder of the Book.

"THINK not that I am come to destroy the law and the prophets; I have not come to destroy, but to fulfil. For verily I say unto you, until heaven and earth pass away, one iota or one point of the law shall never pass away until all shall be fulfilled." These remarkable words have been variously interpreted. They have been referred to the concise summing of the Jewish code, as given by Christ in the two great commandments of love. They have been regarded as denoting the law of nature, as it is called, or the general principles of ethics, as recognized by the conscience. Their interpretation has been found in the ceremonial ordinances as typical, or in the law of sacrifice as fulfilled in its substance by the great sacrifice on the cross. But there is a minuteness, and, at the same time, a universality in this language, that would seem to demand a corresponding exegesis. The *law*, as thus used by our Saviour, and as it was employed by devout souls in the Old Testament, would seem to be another name for God's written revelation—the canon, or "rule he hath given to direct us how we may glorify and enjoy him." Thus received, it would include, even in the present passage, not only the Old Testament Scriptures, but also the words of Christ himself, and all that is revealed by his commissioned messengers as the full complement and development of these older scriptures. God's whole written revelation in the world, from the beginning to the end, the whole canon of Scripture, all that is recognized by Christ as ἅγιαι γραφαὶ or Holy Writings,—"not one iota or one point shall fail." The special words constitute a proverbial expression of universality to denote the completeness of effect. It cannot intend the perfect preservation of the written integrity. There were defective readings and defective translations in Christ's own time; although it is indeed wonderful how, beyond all other works in the world, these writings have been preserved without the loss of an idea, and, we may venture to say, without the change of a figure, notwithstanding all the variations of words and orthography that the keenest criticism has ever collected.

But we may suppose this language of universality to have a wider, and, at the same time, a deeper meaning than either of these views would assign to it. It transcends the

6

rationalistic interpretation, even as it takes in more than any cabalistic veneration of syllables and letters. It embraces the *written word* in its substantial correctness as ever capable of being brought out by fair comparison, whilst it has its truer significance, its more interior significance, in the *living word* as it has been copied in the soul, and printed through ages on the hearts of the Holy People. This is the *textus receptus* that has been carried down on something more durable than parchment. This is the spiritual Mishna, as the Jews called the higher exemplar, or second edition of the law. Every part has been thus *impressed* on souls here or in eternity. A spiritual stereoscope, could we imagine such an instrument, might thus reveal its clear perspective, even though deeply hidden from the common outward view. It is in the memories of the Church militant and triumphant. If lost everywhere else, in every outward form of writing, here is the true spiritual codex, and from this might it be restored, even as it has been said, though it may be hyperbolically, that if all the Bible had been lost as it existed in manuscripts, it might still have been recovered from the Commentaries and devotional writings of the Christian Fathers. It is *the effect* of this written word, we think the Savious means,—the effect of this whole revelation, old and new, first on the Church, and secondly, on the mind and life of the race. Not one jot or tittle shall fail from the law till all be fulfilled. No part shall be without its contribution to this great end. Its history, its poetry, its precept, its prophecy, its genealogies even, will be found to be all necessary parts, not merely of the inception, but of the continuance and the consummation of the work,—all necessary parts of this standing exhibition of God, or the supernatural, in human redemption. And so shall the Bible remain "unto the last syllable of recorded time," the great spiritual power of the world. It shall live until all history shall be seen to be but its fulfilment, and all the divine dealings with our race, from the beginning to the close of its career, to have had constant reference to its "Great Salvation." Nay, beyond this, even in eternity shall it survive. Such would seem to be a fair interpretation of the language on which we are dwelling. "Heaven and earth shall pass away, but not one point of the law shall fail." In this its spiritual power, and in this its ineffaceable spiritual impression, shall it be among "the things that remain," even after God has arisen to "shake, not the earth only, but also the heavens." The present order of nature shall cease, the secular history shall be closed, even the spiritual and ecclesiastical shall be changed, "but the word of our God shall stand forever." Similar to this is the passage Matt. xxiv. 35, Luke xxi. 33—"Heaven and earth shall pass away, but *my words* shall not pass away." The declarations are clearly parallel in their wider significance. The *law*, in the one case, as the known term for all Scripture, and the words of Christ as setting forth its perfect fulfilment, are but different names for one and the same everlasting, unchanging revelation.

A man may find difficulties in the Bible; but surely no intelligent mind can view it without wonder. There is certainly one remarkable change in the aspect of the Biblical question which has been produced by the learned study of late years. Infidelity is as rife as ever; the opposition both of the common worldly, and of the philosophical worldly mind, is as strong as ever; but the age of scoffing has gone by. There can be no more Paines and Voltaires. The days of easy unbelief, as well as of easy belief, have passed away. It is becoming a more serious question, a more earnest controversy for both parties. "*The fight of faith*" is waxing stronger and closer; it is every day presenting, on each side, new and bolder issues. There is, too, this new feature, that each is taking the attitude of assailant. Christianity no longer stands simply on its defence. The war is driven into the enemy's camp, yea, into the very citadel of unbelief. It is shown that the rejection of the Bible is the rejection of all belief beyond the most earthly and sensual. The field of the lists is being narrowed down to the questions—Revelation, or Atheism—Revelation, or the giving up of all hope in a life beyond the grave. The middle ground is being rapidly cleared away, and all who think at all are looking breathlessly for the result of this more than Titanic conflict, when faith shall rise higher than ever, and revelation be more strongly believed than ever, or "Chaos come again" not only in all religious credence, but over that whole firmament of ideas so closely connected with it. The mighty reasoner, Time, is fast bringing to this conclusion the world's best thought. Poetry, Philosophy, Art, all that is spiritual in eloquence, all that is inspiring in nature, all that is stimulating and elevating, even in science, are inseparable eventually from religion, even as religion is inseparable from revelation. They might maintain a lingering twilight existence after its sun had forever set, but must, inevitably, sooner or later, go out in the same overwhelming darkness. In earlier periods of the earth's history they might, perhaps, have longer survived such a "disastrous eclipse," but now, as every reason teaches us to believe, the obscuration would be all the more rapid in proportion to the exhaustion of the conflict, and the depth of the despair.

It is thus that God is putting this question in a way to try the world as it has never been tried before. He who cannot see this is blind to one of the most portentous signs of the times. Even among the most rationalistic and the most sceptical, it is coming to be both felt and acknowledged, that this phenomenon of the Bible and its wondrous hold upon mankind presents a problem requiring for its solution an amount of learning, and a depth of thought, demanded by no other in the history or psychology of our race. What a place that book has occupied in our world! What a blank would have been left, what a blank would now be left, without it! Even the difficulties of belief increase the difficulties of rejecting it. How it lives on in spite of the most startling objections, not now for the first time met, but as clearly seen and as strongly put nearly two thousand years ago as in the present century. It has not only maintained itself, but false philosophies and pretended revelations have obtained a stronger hold in the world, simply by counterfeiting its outward semblance. Thus has it made its way, carrying its own burdens, and the much heavier weights that human depravity has put upon it. Tested by the chances of any mere human conflict, of any philosophic or literary strife, it would ages ago have vanished from the field and been consigned to oblivion; but here it is yet, the mightiest element in human thought, and challenging to the conflict the mightiest of human antagonisms. How it rises up, ever higher and stronger, against every fresh assault! every new phase of unbelief, when it is really new, only calling out some before unknown aspect of power in this exhaustless defence. But it is not enough to say that the Bible has kept its ground in the world ; it has ever been extending itself, not only into new territory, but into new fields of thought. Philosophy assumes to be independent of it, but finds, in the end, that it must go the way of all human speculations, or fortify itself by ideas that can never more belong to human thinking should this book be discarded from the world. So science, too, often "seems first in its own cause, until revelation cometh and searcheth it." Some startling discovery has raised the hopes of unbelief, but soon this more ancient power in the world, this power of the unseen and the eternal, rides over the sense difficulty, or shows it to belong to a lower plane of knowledge with which the diviner truth can have no actual or imagined collision.

It is easy to make objections to the Scriptures,—objections, it may be admitted, extremely difficult of solution,—some of them, perhaps, baffling every attempt at solution; but to explain the strange phenomenon, and the strange history connected with it, this is the great and crowning difficulty that puts all others out of sight. It is comparatively easy to descend into the Avernian pit of infidel cavil, but to ascend therefrom to any clear hypothesis of human destiny after revelation has been once rejected, or to show how certain ideas could ever have been in the world without it, *hoc opus hic labor est;* this is the adventure for which our modern world finds no Hercules; this is the undertaking of which infidelity has not carefully counted the cost, although there are signs of the coming conflict which clearly show that her confident advocates will be compelled to do so. No human intellect—we boldly venture the assertion—no human intellect, and no amount of human learning yet gathered, are competent to the task of accounting, on any known natural principles, for the strange existence in our world of a series of writings, and corresponding influences, so unearthly in their power yet so human in their form, so deep in the world's thought yet so constantly in conflict with all contemporary thinking, and, therefore, at each period of its existence so utterly opposed to any idea of development, —teaching the absolute unity of God through all the black night of the Western polytheism, the vivid personality of God in the denser darkness of the Eastern pantheism, the holiness of God amid every where surrounding forms of worship so impure that they cannot be described, the unrepresentable essence of God when the world was full of a monstrous idolatry or a foul Egyptian symbolism, —proclaiming salvation by the Cross when the schools were priding themselves on the perfection of their ethical philosophy, announcing the resurrection of the body when the select thinkers were soaring in their Platonic spiritualism, and a new and heavenly life for the soul when the vulgar herd of Epicurus were filling the air with the swinish noise of their sensualism,—triumphing alike over the Senecas and the Neros, the Antonines and the Domitians, overthrowing the giant power of ancient Paganism, driving it from that last strong-hold of conservatism it had sought in the philosophic revival of the early myths, shedding a holy light during the long period of Barbarian and Mediæval darkness, breaking forth with new splendor at the Reformation, and yet filling men's minds with fear, or sustaining them in heavenly hope, in the face of a war that never raged so fiercely as in these days when naturalism and criticism combined, as they were never combined before, are doing their utmost to shake the authority of its divine mission.

Every other assumed revelation has been

addressed to but one phase of humanity. They have been adapted to one age, to one people, or one peculiar style of human thought. Their books have never assumed a cosmical character, or been capable of any catholic expansion. They could never be "accommodated" to other ages, or acclimated to other parts of the world. They are indigenous plants, that can never grow out of the zone that gave them birth. Zoroaster never made a disciple beyond Persia or its immediate neighborhood; Confucius is wholly Chinese as Socrates is wholly Greek. But Zoroaster and Confucius, it may be said, were unknown to the world at large, and therefore never had a fair trial. This is true. Their names, indeed, are often in the mouths of the superficial adversaries of the Christian faith, but even now the most learned can hardly claim familiarity with their writings. The question, however, still returns: why have they remained so separate, so powerless out of their own early period, and their own peculiar nationality, unless it be because of their utter want of any world-life or world-ideas, capable of stirring any universal emotion, or producing any universal effect? Why are the remains of these shut up in the libraries of the Archæologist, whilst other Oriental books more ancient still have become household words, and been multiplied in millions and billions of copies through every part of the civilized world? It is a question certainly demanding the most serious study of all who would be thought to take a profound view of human affairs. Writings from the far East, from the earliest East, records almost coëval with the flood, yea, some of them not irrationally supposed to have crossed its world-dividing waters, still taught in the nursery, still read in our primary schools, still taxing all the research of the most learned, still furnishing the fountain source of all that can worthily be called devotion or spirituality in the earth,—giving the child his first ideas of God's creating power, and cheering the aged and the dying with the only hope that can sustain the soul in its dread of the primæval penalty,—the hope that is found in the early, the oft-repeated promise of a conquering Saviour, and the final triumph of redeeming love! What is there that blinds our rational interpreters, so called, to these wonderful aspects of the Bible problem? They are sharp enough to discover everything else but that which so deeply impresses the religious mind, and, without which, the book, though still curious as an antiquarian document, is hardly worth the learned pains they are so laboriously bestowing upon it. Some of them are so keen-sighted that from a few chapters in Genesis, and a few slight differences in Hebrew words, they can give us the chronology of the Weltalter; they can detect the cause of the mistake that assigns Lamech to the last period of the Cainitic instead of his true position in the commencement of the Sethic cycle.* From

* See the Ninth No. of the Jahrbücher der Biblischen Wissenschaft von Heinrich Ewald, 1857, 1858.

these data although so hidden in the letter, their learned and fertile imaginations determine satisfactorily the true relations of the Sethic to the Shemitic Welt-alter ; they know all about the Jahvethum, and the Antediluvian religious sects of the Jahveists and the Elohists ; they can go back of the writer, or writers, and tell us what were the ethnological conceptions which these early "sages" meant to represent in their fragmentary and badly-connected myths ; yea, from their own higher "stand point" they can even concede to them a kind of inspiration, but it is the inspiration of great "historic ideas," which in those primitive times could embody themselves in no other forms but those of a mythical genealogizing. All this they can see very plainly : those primitive sages, they have discovered, were pure idealists ; they were even then thinking out, and expressing, in their mythical way, a Philosophy of History. But the great idea, that which was truly expressed, and has ever since, more or less, affected the world's religious thinking, for this our rational critics have no eyes. They see nothing wonderful in that earliest prediction of the earliest Welt-alter, that the "Seed of the woman shall bruise the serpent's head,"—that one who is divine from his very work, and yet the Son of Man, shall vanquish the power of evil and redeem his suffering brethren from its long and cruel dominion. Wise are they, even above all that is written, in regard to this first twilight of the world's chronology, whilst they fail to understand how this book of Genesis, scanty as are its records, thus furnishes the key to all following history, and discover nothing worthy of their profoundest thought in the fact, that these "myths" of the early and distant East are still exercising such a power over regions, and ages, and manners, and institutions, so different in outward form, so far removed, in space and time, from those to whom they were first given.

CHAPTER IX.

THE UNIVERSALITY OF THE SCRIPTURES — The Bible Compared with other Books — The Paradox — The most *National* and at the same time the most *Cosmical* of Writings — Its World-Life — Its Early Seclusion — The "Going Forth of the Law from Zion" — Sudden and Powerful Effect upon the Greek and Roman World — Hindoo and Persian Scriptures, no Life out of India and Persia — The Koran — Next to the Bible in Catholicity — This comes from its Shemitic Character — Reasons in the Bible itself for its tenacious Life — No Book so Translatable — Other "Sacred Books" shock us by the Monstrosity of their Human — Their Inhuman-*ness* — The Grotesque and Want of Dignity in their Supernatural — In the Scriptures the Marvellous is the Presumptive — The Supernatural becomes Easy of Belief.

THE other writings to which the Jewish Scriptures have been compared never did exert, and never could have exerted such an influence. No historical events could ever have given it to them. It was not from the want of opportunity that their hidden life had been denied its true manifestation. The books of the Bible were originally as secluded as these, yea, more secluded, we may say, more strictly national; but this only makes still more marvellous the mystery of that mighty dominion they exercised, when in God's good time the seals were loosed, and these strange Eastern writings, so unphilosophical, so unlike anything that ever came from the schools, were disclosed to the Western world. For ages had they been shut up in the mountains of Judea, ἔν τινι βαρβαρικῷ τόπῳ πόῤῥω που ὄντι τῆς ἡμετέρας ἐπόψεώς, if we may accommodate that remarkable language of Plato* in which he seems to indulge in something more than a conjecture, that in some distant region, and coming from some distant past, ἔν τινι ἀπείρῳ τῷ παρεληλυθότι χρόνῳ, there might be a wisdom unknown to the Greek and yet to be revealed to the world.(5) There for ages had they remained,

* See the whole of this remarkable passage. Plato Rep. vii.: 498, c. *In some barbarian region far away. In some part of the immense time that is past.*

a "garden enclosed, a fountain sealed," until "the everlasting doors were lifted up," and the commandment came that "the Law should go forth from Zion, and the Word of the Lord from Jerusalem." How sudden, how irresistible the effect! How few the generations before this Chronicle of Redemption, this old Epic of "the Chosen People" and their Hero Messiah, together with those later yet still Jewish writings that contained the world-interpretation of the more ancient national covenant, filled and vivified all the literature, all the philosophy, yea, all the thinking of the vast Roman empire! How soon it modified, yea, completely transformed, that whole historical state out of which arose our modern Europe and our modern civilization! What divine energy was this, that so far surpassed all former powers that had arisen out of the Occidental mind, and might, therefore, be supposed so much better adapted to it? Plato, Aristotle, Zeno, Socrates,—Academics, Stoics, Rhetoricians, Moralists—*they* had never so stirred the world, *they* had touched no universal chords in human souls, although nothing could seemingly be more abstract, and, therefore, more universal, than the language of their precepts. Their speculations, though in appearance so general and so profound, did not, after all, reach down to that which underlies all human nature, as human nature, in its constitution and its wants. They had no Fall to tell of, no Redemption. The former might have been dimly shadowed in some of their poetic myths, but the latter had no place in their philosophy. The world was caring little about them or their systems; it was fast sinking into darkness, with all the light they gave; it was becoming more corrupt, more worthless, with all they said about the excellency of virtue and the dignity of reason; more deformed and false, with all their talk about the "true, the beautiful, and the good." But when Christ and Moses came, when the prophets came, and He of whom they wrote, when Evangelists and Apostles came, how mighty the change, and how soon did it manifest itself in so great a revolution of human ideas! Will some of the men who talk so much of development, explain this mystery that has withstood all the "sneers of Gibbon, and stands yet the inexplicable fact of the world." Development is the magic word; but development from what? From what seed grew this sudden and mighty tree? From what seed in the Greek mind in the Roman mind, in the Jewish mind simply as historically exhibited in the days of Christ, and without reference to any new divine power, or to the spirit of their ancient Scriptures? There is development, surely, a divine development,—involving, however, an effect, and necessitating a cause, than which there could be nothing more opposed to all the ideas the rationalist must assume as the elements of his hypothesis.

And so, too, the Hindoo scriptures, of which our transcendentalists talk so much and so ignorantly, have no meaning, no life out of India. In the West, they have been, and ever will be, but matters of learned curiosity; and even this interest they fast lose the more intimately we become acquainted with them. It would be impossible, by any "accommodations," by any associations, to make out of them a book adapted for any Occidental influence, either moral, religious, or philosophical. It is fast becoming more and more evident that their only theological dogmas of any religious power, or even philosophical interest, are but the almost defaced remains of ideas belonging to the old patriarchal revelation of the World-Deliverer, and which are brought out in all their sublimity in the Christian doctrine of the Incarnation. In all other respects, in their monstrous mythology, in their mind-destroying pantheism, above all, in their revolting impurity, they are what the depraved Hindoo mind has made them, and what they, in their reäction, have made the present Hindoo race. The same local, partial nature may be affirmed, though less strongly, of the Koran. It is a far more catholic book, however,—that is, has more of a world-life, than the Hindoo scriptures; but this comes solely from its Shemitic descent, and from its being such a reflex of the old Shemitic revelation. It would not be far out of the way to regard the Koran as one of the apocryphal books of the Bible. It is from its oft-asserted claim to be the religion of Abraham, "in whom all the families of the earth were to be blessed," that this sublime poem of Mohammed (for with all its falsehoods it is in truth a sublime production) has its real power, its wide-spread, long-enduring hold in so many parts of the older continents.(6) Still, to a great extent, may the same character be applied to all the religious books of the world, except that one which proves its humanity, and so, its true divinity, or the divine in the human, by its universality. Of all the others it may be said that they are local, partial, periodical.

Each has its peculiar phase, chronological and ethnological, out of which it cannot be transplanted. The Bible alone makes disciples of every race. It would be hard to decide where it had more strongly displayed its subduing power,—on the Asiatic, the African, or the European mind. Descending with the ages, and through every phase of humanity, it has met them all, it has warred with all, and its uniform triumph warrants the induction, even aside from faith, that it will surely survive them all. Of such a history it is but sober eulogy if we employ the language of that strange believer, Sir Thomas Browne,—"Men's works have an age like themselves, and though they outlive their authors, yet have they a stint and a period to their duration. This only is a work too hard for the teeth of time, and cannot perish but in the final flames when all things shall confess their ashes."

There is a divine guardianship of the Bible; so we must hold as consistent believers;—

but aside from this, there is in the book itself a reason for its tenacious life. The secret of its lasting hold upon the human mind may be found in this striking union of the closest specialty with the widest universality. Here we have what may be called the paradox of the Scriptures. Addressed primarily to the most separate as well as the most peculiar people on the face of the earth, (and one that still maintains its separateness and its peculiarity, as a standing witness to this remarkable divine economy,) these writings have nevertheless such a wonderful adaptation to all people, to all ages, to all individual men! There must be something in them that goes far below all outward form, all outward dress of age or nationality, something that penetrates the deepest department, the most interior chamber, or *sanctum sanctorum* of the universal soul. They "try the reins;" "they reveal unto man his thought;" "they teach wisdom in that hidden part" where each individual spirit finds its connection, its identity, we might almost say, with the universal humanity. Hence so concrete, and yet so abstract. It is not, however, through logical language, so called, but by the very intensity of their sense imagery, that they pierce through the sense, as it were, "reaching even to the division of soul and spirit," the dividing line of ψυχή and πνεῦμα, and thus becoming "discerners of those *thoughts* and *intents* of the heart" that lie below the ordinary consciousness, but which, when discovered, are recognized to be the most intensely individual, as they are the most profoundly generic, in the human constitution.

Hence it is that no book is so translatable as the Bible. It runs with the least difficulty into all languages, East or West. When it fails to meet with idioms that are perfect equivalents, it will always be found that its own may be successfully transplanted, and that they will grow with surprising freshness and vigor in the new soil. Hence no so ready a way to enrich a language, even an old and copious language, as to translate the Bible into it. We are not generally aware how many of our own most *life-like* idioms are in fact orientalisms thus introduced into our remote Western world. The reason of this may be sought in the seeming paradox before alluded to. It is the "*Living Word*,"* *ὁ λόγος τοῦ Θεοῦ ζῶν καὶ ἐνεργής*, "the Word of God, quick and powerful," yet clothed in humanity ; and hence it is so intensely human because it is the divine in the human. In other words, it could not have been so human had it not also been divine. Only a power high above us could have so looked down into the very depths of our nature. Other or pretended revelations prove their falsehood by their *monstrosity*, by their inhumanness, if we may use such a word, their distorted apprehensions of man, as well as their absurd notions in respect to God. In their ambitious attempts to rise above the human, they get lost in a dreamy pantheism,

* Heb. 4 : 12.

or a grotesque mythology, both of which, while they fall in with a partial order of thought, or a peculiar style of imagination, are alien to the early and natural, to the most uniform and universal, thinking of the race. In the Bible, on the other hand, even the supernatural—we may say it without a paradox—is most natural. It is in such true keeping with the times, with the events and doctrines it attests, with all the surrounding historical circumstances as they are narrated, that we almost lose the feeling of the supernatural in the admirable harmony and consistency of the ideas and scenes presented. It seems to be just what might have been expected; it would be strange that it should be otherwise; the marvellous here is the presumptive, the extraordinary becomes the easy of belief. The supernatural assumes the familiar appearance of the natural, and God's coming down to us, and speaking to us, seem less incredible than that far-off silence which, though so unbroken for our sense, is so perplexing and unaccountable to our reason.

CHAPTER X.

THE BIBLE SUPERNATURAL — Illustrations — The Supernatural at Sinai — The Burning Bush — Moses at the Red Sea — Compare these with the Hindoo, Greek and Scandinavian Myths — The Moral Grandeur — Elijah the Tishbite — The very Natural rising into the Supernatural — The Supernatural in the Life of Christ — Its constant Indwelling Presence — More Impressive than any outward Miraculous Manifestation — "Thou art the Christ the Son of the Living God" — Commands to conceal the Supernatural Power — The Transfiguration — Christ Walking on the Sea — Was it meant for a Display? — Or was it the true Outgoing of an Ecstatic Spiritual Condition? — Mark 6 : 48, "He would have passed them by" — It followed a Night of Prayer — Was this an Isolated Case? — The Scriptures give us but Glimpses even of Christ's Natural Life.

THE thought presented in the close of the preceding chapter receives its illustrations in almost every part of the Scriptures. Its importance demands that they should be given at some length, although it may require for that purpose many consecutive pages. Let us commence with the stupendous exhibition that was made on Sinai. Taken by itself it might seem utterly incredible, although its superhuman grandeur would ever prevent its association with the myths of any other religion. Such a breach in nature, we say, surpasses belief when viewed alone. But when we have read all that precedes, when we have followed on in that flow of events, ever deepening in the intensity of its interest, ever taking in a wider field of vision, ever rising to a loftier region of thought, when the mind has thus become filled with the utmost power of the attending associations, when it is lifted up to the spiritual altitude of the scene, then all things else assume a like elevation ; the darkness and the flames, the fearful thunderings, the quaking earth, the "sound of the trumpet waxing long and loud," even the awful voice, become consistent and probable events ; yea, they would even seem to be natural events. When, moreover, the thought is carried onward to the remote historical consequences of that great announcement of a law from heaven, when we take into view the influence it has exercised and still exercises in our world, then it is that the wonder ceases—we were going to say,—but no, the grandeur, the mystery, the surpassing marvellousness, remain undiminished: it is the *incredibility* that has vanished; for the marvellous, the extraordinary, may be credible, yea, under certain conditions, the most credible of supposed occurrences. When the soul is thus filled with both the *emotion* and the *reason* of the scene, it seems to us just the right interposition, at the right time, in the right way, and for the most rational ends. God proclaiming a law to a people chosen as the conservators of the highest religious truth; what more reasonable than this? His accompanying that proclamation by an outward attesting majesty as shown in corresponding phenomena of the outward physical world; what in itself more credible? Would it not, on the other hand, be something strange to think of, that a world should be created, a race of intelligent and religious beings brought into existence, and that race pass away without any such communication from its unseen maker, without any exhibition of unearthly glory to cast a ray upon its bewildering night of nature, or to relieve the dreary materiality of its long unvaried physical continuance? There are two positions which are out of harmony both for the reason and the imagination: the astoundingly supernatural in the creation of man, the unbroken natural, or the total absence of the superhuman, in all God's dealings with him since. One or the other of these must be given up. The human race is uncreated, or He who made it can speak to it, and does sometimes speak to it. Nature is from *eternity*, or it may be interrupted, and has been interrupted, *in time*. The rejection of the supernatural all the way up to creation, is the rejection of creation itself, both for man and the world. It is well for the truth, that in these latter days of keen inquiry, all untenable middle grounds are clearing up, and the mind is being brought face to face with sharp and decisive issues.

But to proceed with our illustrations; there is, perhaps, nothing in the Scriptures that presents more clearly the holy, religious supernatural in distinction from what may be called the monstrous, or the legendary, than that wondrous sight of the desert, "the bush that burned with fire and was not consumed." On the scale of magnitude and outward force it is surpassed by the convulsions of nature that took place in the deluge, or that attended the descent of God upon Sinai; but for silent grandeur there is nothing beyond it in the Bible. So noiseless and motionless the scene, so calm in its impressiveness,—it would seem, in outward display, hardly to rise above the natural, the strange natural, we may say, that belonged to that remarkable place. The rationalist might, with some plausibility, attempt to explain it as a mirage of the desert. It is its unearthliness, its ghostliness, if we could keep the full power of that old word, that so deeply affects the mind ; like "the still small voice" that came to Elijah, or like Christ walking on the nightly waters when "the disciples cried out for fear, thinking that they had seen a spirit." Such was the effect upon the mind of Moses. The prophet's shepherd life had shown him many weird aspects of nature in that wild region ; he had felt the awe of that lonely spot, held sacred and oracular, even then, from a long antiquity.[7] But this appearance had in it more of the *religio loci* than he had ever felt before. "And Moses said, I will turn aside now and see *this great sight*," המראה הגדל הזה, *visionem hanc magnam*, "why it is the bush is not burned. And the Lord said unto him, come not nigh, put off thy shoe from thy foot, for the place whereon thou standest is holy ground." The poetic interest is, indeed, of the highest order ; there is a sublime beauty in the pictured scene that might vividly impress the imagination of the reader, though without necessarily producing belief. But when there comes forth from the mysterious flame that announcement of the Eternal, "I am that I am,"—I am Jehovah,—"this is my name, and this my memorial to all generations," how perfect is felt to be the harmony between the supernatural and the transcending revelation of which it was made the sign. We allude not here to the mystical or typical, which some, perhaps, would find in the special form of this representation; it is enough for our present view that we simply regard it in its credibility as an act above nature, employed as a witness of the holiest spiritual truth.

Again: When Moses "stretches out his hand over the sea," when he says unto the people, "Fear ye not, stand still and behold the salvation of the Lord," we expect the retiring of the waters; the event as narrated does not surprise us even by its strangeness—it is in such perfect unison with the sustained grandeur of all the acts and all the divine teachings that precede and follow it. But, says the objector, these stories do not surprise us because they are in our Scriptures, which we have been accustomed to regard as full of the marvellous: Has not every nation had its supernatural? were not the heathen myths also believed, and are they not still believed? It is, indeed, true, that every nation has had its supernatural; but this only shows how deeply the tendency to believe it, and to regard it as probable in certain conditions, has its ground in the human soul. The general answer meets broadly, but conclusively, the general objection. In reply to the more special parallel it might be said, that these heathen myths were not believed as the Bible narrations are credited; they are not believed in the same way, they are not believed by the same class of minds, they do not thus retain their hold upon the most cultivated, the most profound, as well as the most religious thinkers of past and present ages. But there is an easier, as well as more conclusive reply. We take the most direct and promptly decided issue. The cases are utterly unlike in their ground statements. There is no resemblance between such narrations as these we have cited from the Bible, and the deformed Hindoo, Greek, or Scandinavian "myths" that some would compare with them. The easy unexamined assumption of such similarity confounds the unthinking and the unlearned; but all investigation proves that the difference is immense, total, we might say, in every aspect. Would we see this resemblance, place them side by side. As Jehovah to Thor, as the Holy One of the Prophets to Vishnu, as the God and Father of our Lord and Saviour Jesus Christ to Zeus, as the Hebrew Prophecy to the Grecian Epic, as the Psalms of David to the Odes of Pindar, as Moses to Minos, as that unique drama in which powers earthly and unearthly are striving for the integrity of Job to the myths of the Æschylean tragedy, as the idea of "Covenant" to the idea of

Fate, as the idea of a Messiah to the idea of a Hercules, as the Olympic games to the "Fight of Faith," so is the sublime supernatural of the Bible to the monstrous, impure, or merely fanciful conceptions of the heathen. The difference is every where,— in the essential reason, in the inward spirit, in the outward form. He that hath eyes to see must see it; he that hath a soul to feel must understand it. We could ask no higher earthly evidence of the unearthliness of the Christian Scriptures than just this parallel. They are not merely arbitrarily selected points. As in the examples cited, so is it with the supernatural of the Bible every where. It is never monstrous, grotesque, legendary, unmeaning, fanciful, but ever dignified, solemn, pure, holy, in strictest keeping with every accompanying emotion, and so preserving that marvellous air of fact, that feeling of truthfulness, that sober impression of reality, that comes from the consistent however high its sphere, and is, therefore, ever present, in the most astounding as in the most ordinary narrations of the Scriptures.

A similar feeling comes over us as we read the story of that lone, fearful man, Elijah the Tishbite? How terrific in its justice, yet how majestic in its consistency, is the divine interposition against the idolatrous priests, when the worship of the true God was dying out in Israel, and but few were known as remaining who had not bowed the knee to Baal! Even we had a religious interest in that remote scene. The natural had come to such a pass as to demand the intervention of the supernatural. The "Lord must come forth from the hiding-place of his power," or the light goes out from the only altar that was to be kept ever burning for the ages and generations to come. But throughout the whole history of this unearthly Seer, what interests us in a most peculiar manner is the striking harmony of the highest miraculous with the simplicity and truthfulness of the ordinary life. What a charm they have for us, and, at the same time, how morally impressive these life-like pictures of the ancient Israel! The Prophet's sojourn "by the brook Cherith that is before Jordan," his journey to "Sarepta, a city which is near unto Sidon," the widow's unfailing cruise of oil, long since passed into a proverbial saying to denote the unfailing providence of God, that graphic scene where Elijah sends his servant to watch from the top of Carmel the signals of the coming rain, the repose under the juniper tree, the heaven-provided sustenance, the Lord's talking with the Prophet at the cave in Horeb, the familiar yet startling question, "Where art thou, Elijah? how life-like is it all! how truth-like in the midst of the most astoundingly marvellous, how minute in circumstantial fact, and yet, with no loss of dignity, no abatement of ever-thrilling awe! And then, that pure religious teaching present in every act! it is this that gives it such a moral consistency, taking away its incredibility, and making it so unlike the *unmeaning* and impure wonders of a false religion.

Thus, especially, does that most remarkable scene in Horeb rise to the very height of the natural as well as the sublime. It is just what we are led to expect,—Deity so holding converse with his faithful servant, the ever-present One thus talking in the solitude of nature to the man who, for his sake, and for his worship's sake, had fled from the world! If it is not so with us in our own personal experience, we cannot help feeling that there must be a lack of that religious intercourse, that personal nearness to God, which would make it seem as probable as it is in itself both rational and true. But how easy, we may say, are such associations of thought and feeling in connection with these striking narratives. The two departments of the world seem to blend together. In its association with the deeply and fearfully religious, the natural acquires a new dignity ; it seems to rise up into the region of the supernatural. On the awful summit of Horeb nature becomes divine ; and we can hardly tell which has most to impress the soul,—the "fire, the wind, the earthquake," or the still small voice that attests the near presence of the higher power. We are lifted up to a plane of thought where much becomes credible that would altogether transcend belief if viewed from the lower horizon of the soul. It is just because the constant reading of the Scriptures produces this elevation of thought, that its miraculous retains that hold upon the Christian faith which the sceptic cannot understand.

But it is in the history of Christ that the idea on which we are dwelling receives its most powerful verification. A life so unearthly, so heavenly, so spiritual, so transcending nature, so full of a divine power manifesting itself in every word and act, so spent in nights of prayer, and days of sublimest teaching! how out of all keeping does it seem, that to a state so earth-transcending in its spirituality, there should be no corresponding witness of the supernatural! There has ever been on the earth some feeling of this kind in respect to men esteemed superlatively holy; but these have been saints just so far as they followed Christ, or were *in Christ*, to use those Scripture words to which nothing else in language is equivalent. Christ was the original power, the fountain of all earthly holiness; He "was the Life," the new transcending life, as it "came forth from the Father into the world." As we read this life—in its natural or unmiraculous aspects we now mean—we recognize the association of the superhuman as we do not in other cases. There is a demand for its presence, as not only a fitting but an indispensable accompaniment. The idea cannot be complete without it. Such power over the soul! it must extend to the body and the physical life; the absence of this healing energy would have been the difficulty to be explained, the feature in the narrative not easy of belief. Such a life and such a death! the resurrection is the only appropriate sequence of a career on earth, yet so unearthly; the ascension into heaven is the only appropriate finale to a drama so heavenly and divine.

The serious reader cannot help feeling that in the life of Christ, as given to us by the Evangelists, there is something more than a supernatural *gift*, or the occasional power of working miracles, as something imparted from without, or only exercised by himself through special effort in each particular case. We are impressed, rather, with the idea of the *constant supernatural*, as a veiled power, not so much requiring an effort for its manifestation as a restraint to prevent it beaming forth before unholy eyes that could not bear, or might profane, the sight. In that earthly tabernacle there was the constant dwelling of the Shekinah, more powerfully present when alone, perhaps, or with a few chosen ones of assimilated spiritual temperament, than in the city or the rural crowd. Such must have been the feeling of the more devout souls admitted to nearest intercourse. "Thou art the Christ the Son of the Living God," is an exclamation called out more by the overpowering effect of this constant presence, than by any great public displays of miraculous power. It is this, more than anything else, that is attested by the holy Apostle John in the beginning of his First Epistle—"That which was from the beginning, which we have heard, which we have seen with our eyes, which our hands have handled of the Word of Life; for the *Life was manifested* and we saw it, and we testify, and tell unto you of that Eternal Life, which was with the Father and was manifested unto us." The reference is not so much to striking outward displays as to the constant spiritual effulgence ever beaming on the soul of the spiritual disciple, and sometimes, perhaps even to the eye of sense, surrounding the person of Christ with an outward glory. From the inward supernatural, as from a never intermitting fountain, proceeded the outward miracle-working power, as exhibited in distinct acts. There is, at times, strong evidence of an effort to veil even these from public knowledge. Again and again are persons charged "to tell no man what they had seen and heard." As the thought cannot be for a moment entertained that this was either affectation or policy, it can be explained on no other ground than the one here taken. Thus, too, are we told of a constant virtue dwelling in the Saviour's person ; as in the story of the woman who "touched the hem of His garment that she might be healed." Her spiritual state, that is, her pure faith, brought her in a living relation to this power so veiled to the unbelieving or merely curious multitude. It was not mere superstition on her part, as some would explain it, or a false feeling, though mingled with some degree of a right faith. Our Saviour does himself sanction her thought when he says (Luke 8 : 46), "For I know that power (δύναμις) hath gone forth from me"—not *failed*, certainly, or *lost*, but spoken of as having flowed forth from himself to some spiritual recipient. We have a Protestant fear of the Romish abuse of this view in their doctrine of relics, and of a wonder-working agency proceeding from the bodies of the saints ; but this fear should not blind us to the clear import of such plain Scriptures. The Romanists ascribe it to dead bodies, to the dead bodies of men who when living had an imperfect personal righteousness ; but here was the Life itself. It is credible, it is even to be expected that the supernatural should shine out through a natural so elevated above the ordinary condition of humanity,—a natural, human indeed to its utmost core, and yet so different from that of the fallen world around it.

There is a deep mystery even in our common physical energy. The strength of the body is, in its ultimate resolution, a power of the quiescent spirit. Activity, force, yea, even, in some sense, motus, or *outgoing energy*, are attributes of soul, even when at rest, as much as thought, or will, or emotion. The present bodily organization, instead of a necessary aid, may be, in fact, a limiting, a restraint upon a tremendous power, that needs to be confined as long as it is joined to a selfish or unholy will, even as we chain the madman in his cell. Sometimes, even in common life, there are fearful exhibitions of the loosening of these material bonds. In the last stages of bodily weakness, apparently, some delirium of the soul, if we may call it such, brings out a power of nerve and muscle irresistible to any ordinary strength, inexplicable to any ordinary physiological knowledge. The cases, indeed, are vastly different, and yet there is some analogy. Such views of the common organism do not at all account for the higher power that may dwell in a perfectly holy spirituality ; but they render it credible ; they prepare us to believe in it, yea, to feel it as a spiritual dissonance if there be wholly lacking some high command of nature in connection with a perfect faith and a holy will ever in harmony with the divine.

It is the Scriptures, however, that must furnish our only reliable ground of argument on this mysterious subject ; and here we find no small proof of such a constant indwelling glory of the supernatural as distinguished from an occasional miraculous gift. In certain passages there is the strongest expression of Christ's unwillingness to gratify curiosity by the display of an outward sign ; in others there is shown an evident reluctance to have this holy influence the subject of any profane or gossiping rumor. But again, he exhibits it of his own accord to chosen disciples, and then it has the appearance of a manifestation, to favored souls, of a power and a spiritual glory ever more truly present in his retired than in his public life. Such is the impression left upon the mind by the account of the Transfiguration. "Jesus taketh Peter, and James, and John, into a high mountain apart (κατ' ἰδίαν). And he was changed," transformed (μεταμορφώθη) before them." The μορφῆ δούλου* could no longer hide the μορφῆ Θεοῦ that was commonly veiled beneath it. "And his face shone as the sun, and his raiment became white as the light." It was that same appearance then, which seems to have become the permanent manifestation of his glory in all earthly visits after his ascension. It was thus that he shone in the vision of Patmos. It was in such a robe of light that he made himself visible to Paul on his way to Damascus. It could not have been merely assumed for the occasion. It was the glory that he ever had, his constant glory, once veiled, but then without a shade. "He was transformed *before them.*" It is the fact of their presence on which, in reading, we must lay

* "*The form of a servant.*"—"The form of God."—Phil. 2 : 6, 7.

the emphasis; this glorious manifestation, not new to Christ, not unusual, perhaps, in his earthly state, they for once are permitted to behold. Peter, and James, and John, are selected to witness one instance of the Saviour's intercourse, it may be his frequent intercourse, with celestial beings and the holy departed. The glory of Tabor may have been often with him in his rapt devotional hours,—a glory known to himself and seen by heavenly eyes. Often may He have talked with Moses and Elias, often "been seen of angels," often had around him "voices from the excellent glory," often heard the chanting of the response, "This is my beloved Son in whom I am well pleased." Could we have the history of Christ as written from the celestial side, his spiritual life as it may one day, perhaps, be revealed to us in the Gospels of Eternity, it might be seen that there were, indeed, many such heavenly visitations, with their heavenly messages, attendant on his nights of prayer and days of holy meditation on the mountain top or in the desert waste.

Something, too, of the same feeling comes over us as we read the account of Christ walking on the waters: "And in the fourth watch of the night Jesus came to them walking on the sea," *περιπατῶν*, or, *as he was walking on the sea.* Not with philological conclusiveness, perhaps, yet still quite strongly, does the participle here suggest the thought of usual or frequent action, of which this was one example, striking, chiefly because of being the one, the only one, that was witnessed by the disciples. We want to give the word the same rendering, and there is no reason why we should not take the thought in the same way as it comes to the mind in Matt. 4. 18: "And as Jesus was walking by the sea of Galilee he saw two brethren." It was not the only walk he had ever taken by the shore of that oft-frequented lake; the impression is rather the contrary, and that, too, as derived from the very form and force of the word, the same in both these examples. On one of these occasions, "he saw two brethren." So here, "In the fourth watch came Jesus unto them *as he was walking* on the sea." Was this a mere wonder-making? Was it done to frighten those timid men? or was it needed, in addition to his other miracles, for the confirming of their faith? There is no evidence that he designed to meet them there for any such purpose. Indeed, the contrary is quite clearly intimated in the parallel passage (Mark 6 : 48), *καὶ ἤθελε παρελθεῖν αὐτούς*, "He would have passed them by," or, "It was in his mind to pass them by," as it may be truly rendered with a clearness and simplicity in strange contrast with the difficulties that a contrary assumption has caused commentators to find in this most plain yet significant passage. But why came he at that hour walking on the waters? Elsewhere, as in Job 9 : 8, it is presented as a peculiar power of Deity,

דורך על במתי ים, ὁ περιπατῶν ἐπὶ θαλασσης, "He who walketh upon the heights, or high places of the sea." It was the sublime, mysterious, spiritual act of a soul in a highly rapt or supernatural state. We might as well ask, Why went he up in the mountain apart? Why, even in the days of his childhood, did he tarry alone by himself when "friends were seeking him sorrowing?" No answer can be given or imagined in either case, that does not refer us to the Redeemer's own subjective state. Why walking thus at that deep time of night over the wild and lonely waves? It was the unearthly act of one filled with unearthly thoughts, and seeking a correspondence to them in the more unearthly, or, as we might even call them, supernatural aspects of the natural world. If the answer cannot well be given in anything out of himself, why should we fear to say that it was a rapt physical state, in harmony with an elevated spiritual frame that demanded it as its fitting outward action?

The ecstasy of the soul lifts up the body. There is something of this in the mere earthly human experience. There is a spiritual condition that seems comparatively, if not absolutely, to loosen the power of gravity, to set volition free, and release even the flesh from the hold of earthly bonds. How much more of this etherial soaring must there have been in the ecstasies of Jesus? In the human spiritual power, as known to us, there is, indeed, nothing that can be strictly compared with it ; and yet there *is* enough to render credible such an absolute triumph over matter in the case of one so holy and so heavenly as Christ. There is an exquisite harmony of thought in regarding the purer etherial element as the appropriate medium, and the undulating waters as the fitting pediment of one so lifted up above the grossness and earthliness of the common humanity.

The writer would be cautious here. On such a subject there is no safety in any speculations unless they keep near to the Scriptures and their fairly suggested range of thought. On this account we may feel the more confidence in noting the remarkable connection of the passage. Thus, we are told in the verse before, "And when Jesus had sent away the multitude he went up the mountain apart by himself to pray, and when it was evening he was there alone." It was in the fourth watch of the night thus spent that Christ went forth in his ecstatic walk upon the sea. The coincidence could not have been a casual one; the inspired writer could not have so regarded it: with all reverence, then, may the reader hold the belief that the supernatural bodily state was not so much a sign, or attesting miracle, as the harmonious accompaniment to the rapt devotion of the preceding hours. Why should not the supposition be entertained that Christ may have often thus walked upon the waters? Of his ordinary or natural life, the Scriptures give us but glimpses; how much more, then, of his extraordinary or supernatural being may we regard as kept beneath the vail.

We think there is no irreverence in such thoughts. At all events, without any special reasoning about spiritual and physical conditions, there is in Scripture itself good evidence that the human nature in Christ was ever in this connection with the supernatural, and that the special miraculous acts were unveilings of a constant hidden power, rather than special enablings or special efforts in each particular case. Christ's own words convey this thought—"He is the resurrection and the life." It is the fair import of the Scriptural language. Even when veiled in human flesh, he is still the *ἀπαύγασμα*, the brightness of the Father, the express image of his hypostasis. "We beheld his glory," says John, "the glory as of the Only Begotten, full of grace and truth." The humanity, too, is a true humanity; no one was ever more perfectly human; and yet so wondrous is he, even in his manhood, that it forces the idea of the superhuman and the supernatural as not only the causal explanation of such an existence, but its own fitting, yea, necessary complement.

CHAPTER XI.

THE NATURAL OF THE SCRIPTURES — A PROOF OF THE SUPERNATURAL — Illustrations — The Antediluvian World — Its Giant Power of Crime — The Patriarchal Life — Its Simple Ethics and Theology — Its "Faith Counted for Righteousness" — How far from the Cloudy Pantheistic Ideas — The Xth of Genesis and it Ethnology — Ewalds' Welt-alter — Joseph — The Israelites in Egypt — Pharaoh and Moses — The Life in the Wilderness — The Heroic Age of Joshua — Days of the Judges — From Samuel to Ezra — We look right into that Old World — Its Vivid Truthfulness — The Prophets — The Monstrous Hypothesis.

AND this presents the argument to whose general statement much of what has been said in the preceding pages is but preparatory. Given the natural in the Bible, the supernatural follows as a logical or necessary consequence; given the credible, or that which is to be received on grounds of ordinary belief, and the marvellous cannot be rejected. Or, to give the statement another form: setting aside, or passing over all that can be called supernatural in the Bible, or leaving it out of view in the first premiss, we have remaining a series of narrations to which no candid man can deny an inherent truthfulness, a strong life-likeness in the delineation of events,—in a word, a rational historic probability unsurpassed by that of any other writings ancient or modern. We say no man can deny this who has truly studied the phenomenon, or has a right feeling of what is deepest yet most human in our human nature. Other religious books, so called, destroy our belief in their supernatural, not more by its own wildness and grotesque monstrosity than by the unnatural and inhuman representations they connect with it of the ordinary or natural life. With the Scriptures it is just the reverse. Aside from the miraculous,—and all this may be taken out without interrupting the history or destroying the earthly consecution of earthly facts,—no narratives are so natural, so human, so inherently credible, as those given to us in the Old and New Testaments.

Turn we first to that most scanty yet most graphic picture of the Antediluvian world. A bare skeleton indeed; but what more probable, what more credible, than that the race, if it ever had any beginning at all, should have had some such beginning, some such introduction into the world, some such early condition as is there ascribed to them. It is true that here the supernatural cannot be wholly left out, for even science forces it upon us; but barely conceding the fact of a creation some way not many thousand years ago, and what a most perfect keeping in all that follows,—the long life of the new manhood, the early fall into evil, the early proclivity to sensualism, the speedy corruption, the mingling of the virtuous and the vile, the greater velocity of the downward earthly tendency, the predominance of the animal after the first rebellion against truth and conscience, the small number of the pious, the few words touching that lonely man of whom the reverence of after years "testified" that "he walked with God and was not seen to tarry long on earth, for God had taken him away,"—the strifes and separations, the great increase of population, the sudden growth of wickedness outwardly accelerated then by the want of that dear-bought experience which teaches men in this old age of the world the prudential policy of individual and social restraint, the giant power of appetite and passion in the early vigorous human frame contributing to the same result, the giant forms of vice, and, perhaps, the monstrous physical births that were the consequence,—the earth at last filled with violence, "all flesh corrupting its way," and hastening on to the utter physical as well as moral ruin, if some power interpose not to save a remnant by the necessary excision of the multitude, and thus preserve a chosen seed for a future and more hopeful world.

How natural, how human, how true to the life, as judged by all we now know of man, or can easily conceive of him in that early time, when sin was young, and passion strong, and the morals of expediency had not yet been reduced to a system on the earth! Can we believe in such a deluge of evil? then is it also easy to believe in that deluge of cleansing waters as the great means both of physical and moral regeneration to a ruined world. The life of man was shortened, but a check was given to that predominating animality which might have reduced our nature to the condition of the brute intensified by the malignity and intelligence of the daemon.

Or turn we next to that postdiluvian patriarchal life, so simple, yet so grand in its simplicity, so religious, as we might well expect men to be after the traditions of such a catastrophe, so fearing God, the One Great God,—El Shaddai, El Olam, El Eliun, Almighty, Eternal, Most High,—and yet with a creed extending so little beyond this prime article, whether we regard it as natural or revealed. "Shall not the Judge of all the earth do right?" This was the substance of their ethics, as well as the sum of their theology. "They were pilgrims and sojourners upon earth;" He who was their God, the "God of the living," was also the God of the pious departed, who in some way, they knew not how, still "lived unto Him." This was the length and breadth of their creed respecting a future state and a future salvation. They trusted in God; "they believed God, and this was counted unto them for righteousness." Such a faith we may concede unto them, and call it natural if we please. It *is* most natural, if by the term we mean that which is most fitting, and, on that account, most credible. It could be shown that nothing would be more *unnatural* than any connection of pantheistic ideas, or of a symbolical polytheism, with that simple patriarchal life. Both are monsters born at a later day, and generated in depraved spiritual conjunctions unknown to the earliest thinking. Let their religion, then, be called the religion of nature; we would prefer, for our argument's sake, to have it so. They believed in God; but beyond this exclude all the supernatural *in act* that has found place in their Bible history. Leave out the visions of angels, the hearing of divine voices, and how truthful is it in all that remains! How strongly does this ancient life impress us with a feeling of its graphic and most intense reality! What mind could have drawn the picture without having drawn from the life, whether that life came to it from tradition or from inspiration!

And so of the collateral records. One may be defied to imagine anything more probable, in itself, than the ethnological chart given to us in the Tenth of Genesis. With what transport of delight would our learned world have received it, how unbounded would have been their confidence in its correctness and its value, had it been dug out of some Assyrian ruin, or decyphered from some crumbling Egyptian monument! A certain modern school has become wonderfully familiar with this early world. They have a sort of intuition that enables them to go up far beyond where Herodotus, and Manetho, and the Bible, and even the hireoglyphics, fail them. There they take their interior post of observation, and think it all out for themselves. Very ingenious are they sometimes; but what German mind so prolific in welt-alter, or what Westminster reviewer can furnish us, from any of their "subjective stand-points," a hypothetical account of the early divisions and races of mankind, more rational, more likely in itself, more perfectly consistent with all known subsequent history, than just the one presented in this remarkable document beyond all doubt so far surpassing any known antiquity.

The same features of inherent verity meet us in the record of the Israelitish bondage, and in that clear page of Egyptian history standing out like some old-world geological relic, we might say, so long before any known chronicles of the later times! Romantic, indeed, but what a life-like romance is the story of Joseph! Strange, indeed, the coincidences, though not more remarkable than have taken place in more ordinary life; but in what other narrative have the good and evil of the human soul been ever blended in such truthful consistency of thought and emotion? been ever painted in such perfect harmony with the universal human consciousness? Take away the dreams, and what has more the air of veritable history, more of that minute detail and circumstantial coloring which the geography and chronology of Egypt could alone impart to it, than the story of the plenty and the famine! We may dispense with Herodotus and the monuments, in our inquiry after the origin of the Egyptian land divisions, and the cast privileges of the priests. Here we have it brightly limned; the traditional copy of Manetho had become sadly defaced in time; we can, however, restore it by the aid of Moses. But let us travel down to a later dynasty, to the days of that new monarch "who knew not Joseph." Look at that world-ideal of the irresponsible tyrant. No fancy ever made him; no human imagination could have kept up a consistency, so well sustained, of character and destiny. Leave out, if you please, all that is miraculous in the plagues, or resolve them into strictly physical events coming at longer seeming intervals, and having a miraculous air by being crowded upon a brief historical canvas. There still remains something that cannot be effaced without effacing human nature. There stand the figures of the prophet and the king; we have before us that truest of despots, that grandest of seers, that pride-hardened heart, that lofty enthusiasm—or, if you please, that stern fanaticism—that burthened people, with their vile, yet most human-like, ingratitude towards their heroic defender, that fearful retribution, that overwhelming fall, that song in the desert, when "the horse and his rider had been cast into the depths of the sea." In the midst of such scenes, as they are presented to the reader's imagination, the avenging angel seems like a demand of nature, and to fall into the rank of expected events. But leaving out, we say, everything of that kind, and where else was there ever presented a narrative of deeds on that high scale so like the truth! The account has become familiar to us, but that is not the secret of its power. Pharaoh and Moses,—we image them, at once, as forms of living men; they have more life for us than Solon and Crœsus, than Socrates and the Athenian judges, than Seneca and Nero, than any characters that were ever drawn by the genius of Homer, or sketched by the graphic pen of Tacitus. The scenes are so vivid, though so far away; so life-like, though of such high proportion; so natural, though so grand, that we can hardly conceive their falsehood. What convergency of scattered myths could have grown into such a consistent whole? What single mind could ever have created a picture so defiant of the antiquating power of time! It has the same life for us now, in this remote Western world, that it had more than three thousand years ago on the banks of the Nile. There it stands right before us, as though written yesterday, clear as the pyramids, fresh as the sculptures on the Karnak, and with a meaning for the world how far beyond any wisdom we may ever hope to get from folios of monumental learning. It is, in fact, a painting that never can grow old; for it is engraved, photographed, we might say, in our human nature; age only adds to the brightness of its coloring; the most minute inspection, under the highest lens of antiquarian learning, only reveals its perfect accuracy of line and shade. Can it be possible that such a *living sketch* could have had no original among the realities of the world?

We pass on to the migration in the wilderness, the rebellion of the people against their prophet, their murmurings against their God, startling to the superficial view, yet how credible when judged by the deeper knowledge of our greatly-depraved, and, with all its powers of reason, ofttimes most irrational humanity. Then naturally rises before us the succeeding epoch, the return of the descendants of the Patriarchs to the old Fatherland, and the divison of the reconquered inheritance. The first chapter in the heroic age is past, and we find ourselves in the days of the "Judges,"—the second race of hero chieftains still filled with the traditional spirit of the earlier day. They were men, and women, too, of mightiest courage, of most lofty enthusiasm; the Scriptures say it was the Spirit of the Lord that came mightily upon them;

but call it what you will, they were just the men and women for the times, and their spirit was just what was demanded for the exigencies of the times, "when there was no king in Israel, and each tribe and family did that which was right in their own eyes." How does each part of the sketch supply the apparent defect of another, until all the portions combined blend into a whole of irresistible truthfulness? The weakness of the mere political bonds, the strength of the ethnological affinities, the civil strifes, the ancestral remembrances holding them together in spite of all dividing causes, the warrior faith of Gideon uniting "all Israel as one heart and soul," the reäction to this high state exhibiting itself in the demagogism of Gaal the son of Ebed, the meaner or unheroic traits that followed the great wars, as shown in "the evil spirit that was put between Abimelech and the men of Shechem," the frenzied curse of Jotham fulfilled in the cruel strifes of the men who had murdered the children of their deliverer, the days of Joshua again called to remembrance by the religious heroism of Jepthah, the lawless Danites who in all their filibustering wickedness must have a priest and a Levite even if they stole him, the terrible fruits of anarchy as shown in the revolting crime of the "men of Gibreh," and that sublime national vengeance which brought together all Israel as one man to punish these sons of Belial and the tribe that refused to give them up,—we see it all; from our distant place of observation we perceive precisely the relations of cause and effect in all their harmonious play and fair analogies as presented to us in these old-world scenes. Their plain chroniclers had no philosophy of history; but they were inspired for a higher office, to set before us a perfect representation of humanity as the materials from which others might construct a philosophy, deep or shallow in proportion as they can enter into the spirit of this strange people, so intensely human, and yet, in many striking respects, so different from all other men.

And then the national history in Palestine from Samuel to Ezra. We venture the assertion, that never in the annals of the race has there been so much of nature, of pure humanity, yea, of the most important historical ideas, so compressed, yet so graphically given, in the compass of so few pages. There is a light in truth, a self-evidencing light, that helps us to see across that wide chasm of centuries ; we discern objects plainly on the other side ; we look right into that old world ; so perfect is the diorama that we see it to be a real, living, moving world, with a wondrous life impressing us with a sense of its distinct reality more strongly, perhaps, than any page that comes nearest to us in our own most modern history. To come down to later times, what can be more stirring, more like a veritable, undeniable thing, whose falsehood, when once the image has been distinctly formed, it is more difficult to conceive, than the rapt enthusiasm and burning harangues of the Jewish prophets. We refer now to their subjective state as an intense human reality, irrespective of any supposed supernatural cause, or of any assumed truth of their predictions. In those impassioned appeals the whole national and genealogical history comes over again. About this time, as some hold, the Pentateuch and the earlier parts of the Old Testament were written, in other words, the whole Jewish history created. But what a monstrous proposition this! When carefully examined, or even barely looked at, can anything surpass it in improbability, did anything ever come from the learned lovers of paradox, that presented such a demand upon our credulity? We must imagine the almost unimaginable absurdity of a whole national legislation, with all the manners and peculiarities and modes of thought that might be supposed to grow out of it in the course of ages, a national archæology full of supposed glorious reminiscences, a national poetry seemingly inspired by these shadowy nonentities, a national didactic or ethical literature seemingly grounded on such a baseless ancestral wisdom, a national culture hypothetically the growth of historical centuries that never had any existence, or any adequate existence for such a purpose,—we must imagine all this, we say, from Genesis to Ezra, to have been a compilation, if not an entire forgery, of the latest prophetic period itself, or else the Hebrew prophets give us the most truthful as well as the most animated picture of a national life that was ever painted in the annals of the world.

CHAPTER XII.

The Internal Truthfulness of the Scriptures — Three Hypotheses — 1. A Veritable History — 2. An Entire Forgery — 3. A Traditional Compilation — The Second Impossible — Reasons — Peculiar Character of Historical and Literary Forgeries — Wholly Alien to the Idea of that Age — If the History Forged, how much must be Forged with it — The Third Hypothesis — Imagined Method — Difficulties — Unfitness of the Later Times of Jewish History for such a work — Still it is Plausible, unless there is some Internal Obstacle — There is such an Obstacle — How History arose in Other Nations — Might be so Regarded as arising from the Jewish, were it not for a Peculiar Trait — The Bible a Book of Numbers — Compare the Pentateuch with the First Volume of Grote's History of Greece — Driven to the first Hypothesis.

Let us dwell on this, for it is deserving of our most attentive consideration. The study of the Bible, as it ought to be studied, brings us to a sharp and unavoidable issue. The Jewish histories are the most astounding of forgeries, or they are the most truthful writings the world has ever seen. This can be made clear by simply presenting the only three theories that can possibly be had respecting them, and which may be thus stated:

1st. It is an authentic and veritable history, written, as a whole, and in all its parts, at the time or times at which they purport to be written, and by persons having a near knowledge of the events recorded, whether that knowledge came from inspiration, or personal acquaintance, or accurate tradition carefully preserved and capable of being tested by its close contiguity with the acts recorded, on the one hand, and the first recording chronicler, on the other.

2d. It is an entire forgery, made in the later periods of the Jewish nationality in order to give to it an ancestry and antiquity to which in truth it had no claim,—all its details being sheer invention,—its archæology, its chronology, its geography, its political and social delineations being the work of some single mind or minds conspiring for that set purpose, and setting themselves deliberately to the work of so minute and comprehensive a falsehood.

3d. It is a compilation made in the latter days, but from sources existing before. These are traditions and fragmentary records, of which the latter are to a good degree, though not entirely, mythical, and the former had grown out of obscure ancient events, having some ground of truth, and so honestly believed, but exaggerated from age to age, with a continual addition of the marvellous and the supernatural, until at last their growth was checked by their being incorporated into a more comprehensive and methodical history.

One of these is true, for here are the books; here is the Jewish nationality, as it has been for ages crystallized in the very heart of history. The first, then, we say, is possible, involving no absurdity (even if we connect the supernatural with it), and must be received as against the second, or if the issue is confined to them alone. The second is utterly incredible, unimaginable in design, impossible in execution. No one would even think of it, who has formed any conception of what it actually involves. The third is probable, natural, apparently consistent with what is known of the formation of other early history, and would have a fair claim to be received, if there is no higher opposing evidence, or if there is not something in the Bible history that altogether shuts out any such comparison with apparently corresponding annals of other nations. That there is something of this kind, and that, too, patent on the very face of the Jewish Scriptures, we think can be clearly maintained. In short, there is a serious difficulty in the plausible *third*, which, equally with the utter impossibility of the *second*, drives us back to the *first* as the only hypothesis consistent with nature and truth.

The absolute, wholesale forgery must be rejected. It is incredible in itself; it is incredible from the outward difficulties that must attend such an undertaking. It is inherently incredible. No motive can be assigned for it. Let us imagine it, if we can. Let us carry ourselves back into the period supposed, with all its surroundings, as far as they may be known from other sources ; let us try to think of some single scribe, or some number of scribes, in the days of Hezekiah, preparing pens and parchment rolls for such a purpose, even to impose upon a nation a history unknown to the national life, a religion and a worship unconnected with any previous sentiments either of reverence or superstition. The very difficulty of the conception shows the far greater difficulty of anything like success in the execution. The story of Samson is far less incredible ; the worship, by the Jews, of the Egyptian Apis, or of the calves of Jeroboam, would be even less irrational and absurd. Historical and literary forgeries belong to a peculiar state of things very different from anything we can conceive of as existing among the Jews in the days of Ezra. There is ever some wide age-agitating interest, some sharply controverted world-idea, to which they are brought in aid. It is on this account that they are ever collateral, never wholesale; ever fragmentary, partial, remote, avoiding direct connection with the present state of things, never creating *de novo* not only the collateral aids but also the entire cause to which they are brought in aid. Hence they are ever assigned to an antiquity cut off by deep intervening chasms from any present emergency they are cited to explain. Thus the forgeries charged upon the Patristic period were broken Sibylline verses, or scraps of oracles; they were fragments from the days of Orpheus, as was supposed, or the Egyptian Trismegistus. But these Jewish forgeries must be forgeries all the way down to the days of the forgers. They connect themselves with an immediate past of which they to whom they are addressed have no knowledge. They are wholesale, too, as we have said ; they must include, and do include, if this most difficult theory be correct, not only a forged history, but along with it a forged poetry, a forged national literature, a forged ethics, a forged religion, a forged worship, forged prayers and hymns, a forged ritual system all made to suit, forged national songs for forged deliverances, a forged geography, at least in its names as adapted to ancient local events, a forged chronology, together with the forgery of many thousand proper names of men all having a significance in the vernacular language, and that significance corresponding so wonderfully to the times and circumstances in which they are supposed to be given. Even the language itself must, to some extent, be forged ; it must be cut over like an old garment and made to fit the earlier as well as the later body. Old words must be forged, and obsolete grammatical forms, and obscure passages made on purpose, such as to demand the Scholiast's aid, and all this by men in whose language there had been previously no writing, no books, no literature, and, of course, no means of culture either for the individual or the common mind. We cannot receive this. The Jews *had* books, they had varied writings, they had a poetry, a history, a religion, they had schools and public teachers, they had men who wrote and were known as writers, they had all this in the days preceding Ezra, and must, therefore, have had it long before, and we must believe that they had it, just as their history implies, or else admit all these absurd and impossible ideas.

There is a story of a man, and of some learning, too, who maintained that all we have, or seem to have, of classical antiquity, was a wholesale forgery committed by some monks of the middle ages. It was not so extravagant as this idea of a Jewish forgery, inasmuch as there is in the Jewish nationality and its collateral life a much more truthful coherence than we find in Greek and Roman history. It is less extensive indeed, but loftier in its aim, far deeper in the grounds and consistency of its national existence.

But why dwell upon this view? It is not only incredible; it is utterly impossible, and the idea is to be dismissed at once. We believe that no man of standing as a scholar or a thinker now really holds it, however much he might be willing to give such an impression favor with the common mind. The more thoughtful among the German rationalistic interpreters see its utter absurdity, although some of their speculations can be maintained on no other basis. In short, take all the Old Testament supernatural, separate or combined, and it cannot present a problem so hard for our understanding, or a statement so difficult for our faith, as this hypothesis when carried out in all its legitimate deductions.

There remains, then, the first view, unless there be some good ground for resting in the third. Is the Jewish history a compilation?—not a forgery, but an honest gathering of national traditions, and some few isolated and fragmentary records made from previous traditions, though none of them, except perhaps those that belong to the latest times, coming from persons contemporaneous with, or near in time to, the events narrated or recorded? A mere recension of writings all existing before, though now arranged in order, would not suit the hypothesis. It would not differ enough from the common view of the scriptures to make a difference of argument. Historical traditions having a strong outline character, national laws and customs connected traditionally with supposed early events, these events thrown into an unknown antiquity, regarded indeed as old, but with an absence of any definite or consistent chronology,—add to these local traditions, family traditions, together with some few writings of a lyrical rather than a documentary character, songs of war or hymns of devotion, with here and there, perhaps, a monumental record rudely carved on rock or temple, and we have just the materials for our third view and the arguments demanded for its consistency. The question then is, did such a work of compilation, or gathering and shaping of all floating historical element, take place in those later times to which some would give the name of known or authentic history, (even calling it "the historical" emphatically in distinction from the mythical,) although it is, in fact, just that period of the Jewish nationality which is the least known and most confused of all.

It is certainly a very remarkable thought, not indeed wholly subversive of this view, but suggested immediately by it, that the beginning of a nation's written or authentic history should be the beginning of that portion which is the darkest in its entire annals. For such—in the subjective effect, certainly, or the truthfulness of its impression—is the character and position of the four or five centuries of Jewish history between the captivity and the coming of Christ. It stands like a dark hiatus between the clear pictures of the Old and New Testament; on either side a well-defined and cultivated territory, between them a pathless and tangled forest. What a light is there about Moses, and David, and Solomon, and Hezekiah, and Isaiah, as compared with Onias, and Hyrcanus, and Aristobulus, and other dark figures that flit about in the chaotic waste over which, even with the aid of Josephus, we find it so hard to make our way. Every reader of this last named author must have felt something of this. How sudden is the transition, and how sensible we are of it, when he passes from the known field of the canonical writings! It is as when the traveller leaves the fertile land, or the border of the green oasis, for the arid Sahara. If the Jewish written history first commenced with this period, then was the morning the beginning of the night.

But waving all these considerations, let us proceed with the hypothesis, and see what its completion involves. In the days of Ezra, then, or within a generation or two either way, some of the wiser men of the Jewish nation sat themselves down to this gathering of the national memories before they should be forever lost. They talked with the old fathers of every tribe, they visited monumental places, they examined carefully the scattered current traditions, they hunted out every written scrap they could find of the national songs; they listened to the Prophet or poet, the Hebrew Ish Elohim or inspired "Man of God," the *Θεῖος ἀνὴρ*, or national bard, as he chanted the old unwritten melodies, or those peculiar Messianic Oracles in which this strange race had ever claimed for themselves a world-destiny; they looked into the traditions of other neighboring nations supposed to be remotely though genealogically allied, and through them endeavored to ascend to a higher patriarchal age, giving themselves the rank of First Born among the Sons of Men. These materials they endeavor, as well as they can,—but with all honesty,—to get into some chronological order. This would be, indeed, their hardest task, but having succeeded in it, as they supposed, with tolerable fidelity, though necessarily leaving much unknown and still more that was utterly irreconcilable, they next supply, but honestly supply, from their best conjectures, the old national ideas, religions, laws, that could alone account for such remarkable traditions, and for such a peculiar attitude as they must be conscious of having toward the other nations of the earth. Now in all this we have supposed them honest; for it is, in fact, essential to the integrity of the hypothesis, and becomes of great importance to the question whether the Jewish history as we have it now lying in our Bibles could ever have been *compiled* by truthful men from such materials, and to the still further and involved question whether, therefore, this third of our suppositions does not, after all, contain a difficulty equal to, if not still greater than, anything in the second. Still they might be honest, and yet exaggerate. They might have no idea of direct or systematic forgery, and yet the national pride might lead them unconsciously to give a coloring to certain traditions, and perhaps, without intending any cheat, to enhance the marvellous that had already been growing through ages of successive transmission.

As an *a priori* supposition, then, this third scheme, as we have presented it, and very fairly presented it, we think, looks extremely probable. If we had never opened our Bibles to see how strange a history they actually contain, how different from that of any other ancient nation, we should regard it as a most rational mode of accounting for the matter. There is an inherent plausibility in the thing; it is so like the way in which history may have arisen among other peoples, that we are inclined to receive it if there be nothing in the way, no formidable obstacle, at least, in the very history supposed to be the result of such a process.

But there is something in the way; there is just such a formidable obstacle. If they have produced this history we now have in our Bibles, then the *compilers* of these Jewish annals (if they are but compilers) cannot be so relieved from that charge of direct, palpable, and *conscious* forgery which we find it so difficult to believe of them, and for the sake of avoiding which this third hypothesis was resorted to. There is that peculiarity in the Jewish Scriptures, and in the Jewish history throughout, which brings into the third scheme all the difficulty, or the greatest difficulty, of the second, and that, too, without its consistent boldness of design and execution. It is not hard to conceive how the early Greek history thus grew up, or the Greek myths as they may well be called, and how they were afterwards arranged in the best chronological order and political method that could be obtained from such chaotic materials. It is all very much as we should *a priori* expect to find it; gleams of light appearing here and there, a few consecutive lines of historical strata running on with tolerable clearness and consistency, then interrupted by sudden *faults* or abrupt interminglings which no clue that we can find enables us either to separate or unite,—a chronology in perfect disorder, sometimes, by reason of its overlappings, running up to a pretentious and impossible antiquity, again, by reason of some vivid impression it had made, bringing some very ancient event away down into the very foreground of these mythical groupings. And so of all the early stories given by Herodotus, as derived by him from the priests, and poets, and popular traditions of the various nations that he visited. The very cloudiness that surrounds them, the disproportions of arrangement, the predominance of the fanciful obscuring and sometimes putting beyond all recovery the idea or historical fact they might be supposed to represent, the legendary features every where prevailing, the manifest air of the marvellous and the extraordinary unrelieved by pictures of the common and familiar life, the unmistakable aim of the chronicler or traditionist to call attention to the mere wonder whilst casting in the back-ground the moral or religious lesson whose prominence in the Jewish "myths" gives the supernatural the subordinate place, and thus, as we have shown before, imparts to it its air of strange and almost supernatural credibility,—all these things, as we find them in the earliest accounts of other nations, are just as we expect. There is just that misty, magnifying, distorting, wonder-making, legendary, mythical air, confounding all chronology, and all geography, that absence of dates, that confusion of places, that blending of events far distant from each other in time and space, which show the want of all attesting means of knowledge, whilst they bear witness to the fertile imaginations, the excited feelings, in fact, the subjective truthfulness of these mythical story-tellers, as it appears in the very disproportions and exaggerations of their narratives. Instead of having any accurate chronicles of years, these λογογράφοι do not even make any pretence to it; they would seem to have regarded any such precision of places and times as at war with that feeling of the wonderful that filled their minds, and which dwells chiefly in the vast and the obscure.

Such is all ancient mythical history, and we are not surprised to find it so. Nothing but some supernatural knowledge and supernatural guidance could have made it otherwise. But such is not the scripture history, either in its earliest or latest stages, and whether we regard its narratives as traditions or as having been the subjects of recording at the time of occurence. The moment we open these "Jewish myths," so called, there is discovered a most remarkable difference lying patent on every page. This peculiarity, so obvious to the least reflecting reader, is what may be called the *statistical* character of the Scripture Chronicles. The Bible is a *Book of Numbers.* It is a trait maintained consistently throughout. From the exact nativities of the Antediluvian ages, from the precise dates of the rising and subsiding waters of the flood, from Noah's almanac, as we may say, down to Haggai's diary, or careful noting of the very year, and month, and day of the month, in which the word of the Lord came unto him, it is all of a piece, one consistent number-giving, time-keeping record. The Jews, if there is any truth in their history at all, were a journalizing people, a genealogizing people; the Bible is their family book of entries, just as we now employ certain pages of it as a register of births and deaths. Precise statistics are every where, and every where purporting to be from men who knew, and who are, in the main, supposed to be recording known present or passing facts. There is nothing like it in the history of any other people on earth; certainly not in any early history. All the way up to the flood, with a few gaps which seem to have been left designedly to baffle human curiosity, there is a regular chronological track.

Now let any one compare the first volume of Grote's History of Greece with the Pentateuch, the confused and utterly unchronological annals of the Doric, Hellenic, and Eolic races, with even the earliest part of the Mosaic writings, or the history of the Patriarchs, and he will see at once the difference on which, in view of its most important consequences, we are so strongly insisting. Darkness, confusion, shadows, deformities, painful perplexities, or hopeless riddles, in the one,—the clear geography, the direct chronology, the fact consistency, the life-like minuteness of coloring, the strange combination of the marvellous in such perfect affinity with the familiar and the domestic that it loses its marvel,—all this in the other. Even after the commencement of what is called the "historical period," or the introduction of the Olympiads, the Grecian chronology is full of obscurities. It is not easy to fix the times of the historians themselves; there is a doubt about Herodotus; the Heraclidæ and Lycurgus fail of being precisely determined by some centuries; but more than a thousand years before Herodotus, the Hebrew writings set forth a regular chronology. Before Hellenians and Dorians had set foot in Greece, many centuries before even the Pelasgi "were in the land," we are told the time of life, and have the means of reckoning the very year, when Abraham went forth from Ur of the Chaldees. No, there is no escape from it: the Jewish history is the boldest of lies, the most unscrupulous of forgeries, and, at the same time, the most inexplicable of literary enigmas, or it is *the truth*, attested inwardly and confirmed outwardly, as no other ancient historical account was ever attested in the multiplied annals of the race.

CHAPTER XIII.

THE ARGUMENT CONTINUED — STATISTICAL CHARACTER OF THE SCRIPTURES — The Antediluvian Genealogies — The First Obituaries — The Dates and Numbers of the Deluge — Its Graphic Description — The Gradual Rising — The Scene Pictured by an Eye-Witness — The Minutely Inventive Style belongs to Much Later Times — The Most Truthful of Narratives or the Most Monstrous of Lies — Subjective Truthfulness — The Jewish Year — Its Early and Remarkable Accuracy — More Acurate than the Greek or Roman — The Weekly Division of Time — Purely Shemitic in its Origin.

IN the very beginning of Genesis, in the very frontispiece, we may say, of the whole Scriptures, we find this statistical character. "And Adam lived an hundred and thirty years, and begat a son in his own likeness, after his image, and called his name Seth ; and all the days that Adam lived were nine hundred and thirty years, and he died. And Enoch lived sixty and five years, and begat Methusaleh ; and Methusaleh lived an hundred and eighty and seven years, and begat Lamech ; and Methusaleh lived after he begat Lamech seven hundred eighty and two years, and begat sons and daughters ; and all the days of Methusaleh were nine hundred and sixty and nine years, and he died." And so on through the births and deaths of this old Antediluvian Patriarchy. There is, too, a moral lesson here, impressive and sad, and giving to these dry numbers a sublime moral dignity. It is not obtrusive, indeed ; it is not suspiciously forced upon the notice ; to the dull reader these details and repetitions may seem as barren as the fragment of Berosus, which is evidently an imitation of this older document ; but to the man whose spirit is awake, it is the solemn record of execution on the great judgment pronounced in a previous chapter ; it is the commencement of that long death which our humanity has been dying ever since. It is the first great obituary, recorded, not on blank, intervening leaves, but "*in capite libri*," in the beginning of "the volume of the book." It is the title-page to that *true* history of the world, written on the tombs, and preserved where all else perishes, even in the dust of the earth.

There is the same character, though carried to a still farther degree of graphic minuteness, in the account of the Deluge. We have the exact year, the month, the day of the month, when the great rain commenced upon the earth, and Noah went into the ark. Were ever the pictorial and the statistical combined in so life-like a description?

"On the self-same day entered Noah, and Shem, and Ham, and Japhet, the sons of Noah, and Noah's wife, and the three wives of his sons with them, into the ark; and the flood was forty days upon the earth; and the waters increased and bare up the ark, and it was lift up from the ground; and the waters prevailed and were increased greatly upon the earth, and the ark went (וַתֵּלֶךְ walked forth, ἐπεφέρετο) upon the face of the waters; and the waters prevailed exceedingly upon the earth, and all the high hills that were under the whole horizon were covered; fifteen cubits upwards did the waters prevail after the mountains (or the highest hills) were covered. And all flesh died that moved upon the earth; and Noah only remained alive and they that were with him in the ark; and the waters prevailed upon the earth an hundred and fifty days." Surely the man who first painted this scene must have been in that ark when it was "lifted up," and went walking forth upon the waters; he must have been an eye-witness of that irresistibly rising wave, those disappearing hills, all ending at last in that sky-bounded waste. "Under the whole heaven"—who that has any true love or reverence for the Bible, would raise an argument, on these words, either for or against the absolute universality of the deluge, or think of interpreting the writer at all by either our modern geography or our modern astronomy! It was all of earth he knew, or that was known to Moses after him. The divine Spirit that employed his vivid conception, as well as his vivid language, has given it to us as the measure and the assurance of his truthfulness. The absolute geographical extent is to be determined by other proofs and other passages. But here we have that which filled the writer's eye; it was the optical carried out to the fullest extent of the known or the imagined; and it is just that truthfulness which, in such an account as this, is of the highest critical value. He who deals with it in any other way, ruins one of the most precious evidences of the Scriptures. It will bear no scientific reconciliation; it utterly rejects the aid of any rhetorical addition. We may be chargeable ourselves, to some extent, with the very fault here imputed; still are we deeply conscious that any attempt to put the account in other language than that of this eye-witness, and especially as it lies in the inimitable Hebrew, only mars the picture. They are the words of that high emotion, that calm emotion, we might say, that could not bear exaggeration ; it is the utterance of that clear spiritual impression that shapes its own first language, never to be improved by any other.

In perfect keeping, too, is the account of the subsiding flood. Let the infidel look up his favorite story of Deucalion and Pyrrha, and see, if he is capable of seeing, the mighty difference ; let the rationalist read over again his Hindoo myths of the deluge, and be utterly ashamed of his comparisons. "And God remembered Noah, and every living thing, and all the cattle that was with him in the ark ; and God made a wind to pass over the earth, and the waters assuaged ; the fountains also of the deep and the windows of heaven were stopped, and the rain from heaven was restrained ; and the waters returned from off the earth *continually;* and after the end of the hundred and fifty days the waters abated." "*Returned continually*," הלוך ושוב "to go and return," "going and returning;" such is the expressive idiom of the Hebrew; it is most pictorial language, and denotes a sort of ebbing subsidence having its intervals of standing and sinking until it reaches the lowest and settled state. "And the ark rested in the seventh month, on the seventeenth day of the month, upon the highlands of Ararat; And the waters kept going and retiring הלוך, וחסור *ibant et decrescebant*, until the tenth month: in the tenth month on the first day of the month were the tops of the mountains seen," *apparuerunt cacumina montium*. The utmost intention of plainness and simplicity cannot prevent the language from rising into the poetical. "And it came to pass at the end of forty days that Noah opened the window of the ark; and he sent forth a raven which went to and fro (*Heb.* going out and returning, or, back and forth) until the waters were dried up from off the earth. Also, he sent forth a dove from him to see if the waters were abated; but the dove found no rest for the sole of her foot, and she returned unto him in the ark, for the waters were on the face of the whole earth; then he put forth his hand and took her, and pulled her in unto him into the ark; and he staid yet other seven days, and again he sent forth the dove out of the ark; and the dove came in to him in the evening, and lo, in her mouth was an olive leaf plucked off; and Noah knew that the waters were abated from off the earth; and he staid yet other seven days, and sent forth the dove which returned not again unto him any more. And it came to pass in the six hundredth and first year, in the first month, the first day of the month, the waters were dried up from off the earth: and Noah removed the covering of the ark, and looked, and, behold, the face of the ground was dry; and on the second month, on the seven and twentieth day of the month, was the earth dried."

How can any serious soul fail to be struck with this strange combination of the minutely familiar and the inexpressibly sublime? To think of a man's deliberately sitting down thus consciously to forge all this numerical exactness, and yet preserving that other awful feature so inconsistent with the meanness and littleness of known and intended lying! For such, if it be not strictly true, must have been the character of this account when first written, unless thus filled in by our supposed compilers. A wilful forger, earlier or later, could not have so described it; he must have betrayed the untruthfulness of his position. A mere wonder-making traditionist could not have given us the story in a manner so different from that of the early Greek logographer, or Hindoo mythopœist; the legendary would have manifested itself; for that *art of* fictitious writing, which could alone have kept back its untruthful aspect, was not invented until ages after, and has only in the latest times arrived at its perfection. Yet nothing in the most modern times, whether fictitious or real, could surpass it in this air of simple verity. We cannot avoid being struck with the unpretending calmness, the simple majesty, the utter absence of the swelling, the pretentious, the wonder-showing, in a narrative that relates such marvels. An account in one of our newspapers of an inundation of the Mississippi shall have ten times the air of hyperbole, shall go utterly beyond it in all those turgid features of narration which betray on the part of the writer the feeling that he has something very great to tell, and an evident delight in making his readers share in the same emotion. For a *truthful* man, thus perusing the account of the flood, it is difficult to divest the mind, at least for the moment, of the idea of the substantial *subjective truthfulness* of the story itself. We mean by this, its perfect honesty as reflecting the honesty of the first narrator, however defective he might be in science, or however mistaken in regard both to the natural and supernatural causality. He narrates things as he *saw* them and *felt* them; he gives us truly the *appearances* and the *emotions*, the latter not as subjects of introverted description, but as exhibited in the style and language called out by the phenomena. This is enough for our present argument; when it is complete and carried throughout the Bible, then let any one resist the impression of the supernatural, if he finds it easy to do so. But in reading this story, so simply yet so grandly told, we are impressed, as by a real passing scene, with the belief that there actually was such a man as Noah in the early world, a very righteous, honest man, who had on his mind, whether deceived in his idea of inspiration or not, a real conviction that there was coming such a flood of waters over the whole known land, that, under the influence of this belief, he built a vessel, that he took into it his family and the known animals of the surrounding country, that in all this he religiously regarded himself as prompted by a divine power, that the waters did come, that they rose gradually as is so graphically described, that they as gradually abated, that he sent forth the dove, that she returned with an olive leaf in the evening as is so touchingly told, that he "put forth his hand and took her and pulled her in unto him in the ark," that "he waited other seven days," and finally came forth from the ark on that very month, and day of the month, of which he had made so careful a register for those who were preserved with him, and for the sake of those who should be after him upon the earth. How monstrous the lie if it be not the honest truth! We mean not, how monstrously false in its marvellous, but in its minute dates and details, in those *circumstantial lies* that must have been all along accompanied with such a consciousness of falsehood on the part of the narrator. The marvellous might have grown from some traditionary small beginning, and the first writer been very honest in his belief of it:

we can easily understand that: it would be no impeachment of the logographer's truthfulness, but rather a proof of it, had he allowed the wonderful to make some increase of magnitude in his own mind, and thus been led to bring into the narrative rather more of the supernatural than it possessed when it came to him. Such a natural growth is easy to be conceived; but the other idea is quite incredible,—we mean, except on the supposition of its being an absolute and entire forgery, where invention becomes natural and predominant. Traditionists, or the chroniclers of traditions, do not thus conspire. They may enlarge, but they do not thus minutely fill up; for the very consciousness of what they are doing must destroy their belief in the story, and take away from them that character of subjective truthfulness which the supposition demands. The human inventive faculty may, indeed, go a great way, but it is not employed in such a manner, and from such a motive. Its end is amusement, sometimes, the exhibition of its power, or there is some collateral purpose which cannot be conceived of in such a case as this. The minutely inventive fictitious style of writing is an art of slow growth. From such clumsy beginnings as we find in the earliest efforts, more unnatural in fact than the wild mythical legends that aim at no such character, they require ages to bring them to that easy finish which is now sought for in this kind of composition. In fact, the Defoe style belongs to the very latest period of the world's literature, it is a species of Flemish painting that comes after the great old masters ; it is an introversion of human powers seeking a new occupation when the sublimely truthful, or the simple in history, as well as the sublimely marvellous, had ceased to charm. The supposition that it existed in the days of Moses, or for a thousand years after Moses, is more incredible than any thing for which it may be brought to account. It is utterly inconsistent with any feeling, or motive, or state of mind, that we can imagine for those early days. It must have a consciousness of falsehood staring it in the face with every unit, and ten, and hundred, it employs, and this debasing effect is directly at war with those sublime religious conceptions, whether true or false, that are mingled with it.

Every reader of the Bible must be familiar with the great number of other examples that might be given of this same statistical character. There is the Jewish year, presenting quite a question for the learned, if they will but carefully look at it. The adjustment of the current annual time had a difficulty for the early days, of which we can form some conception when we bear in mind that our familiar almanac knowledge has been, in fact, the growth of centuries. But this unscientific people seem to have settled this problem, at least for all practical approximations, or to have had it settled for them, even before the Exodus. Ever after, the calendar of their months and festal seasons seems to have had almost the modern accuracy, while the Greek and Roman year remained for centuries later in great confusion, and the Egyptian, if we may judge from what is said by Herodotus, was hardly in any better state. The intercalation of five days, the best method then known, must have produced a disorder of nearly a month in a century. The Israelites had certainly some better way. The learned Arabian Makrizi, who goes very fully into the matter, gives us an account of the methods employed by the later Rabbins, but these could not have produced the remarkable accuracy that must have existed in their festival-keeping before the captivity. A mere observation of the new moons would not have kept their time from floating if there had not been some method of fixing the solar year, whether from astronomical means, or some unerring signs of vegetation.

If this calendar accuracy, as we may call it, had stood out by itself, an isolated characteristic, there might be some plausibility in regarding it as a forgery of a later age. But it is in keeping with the whole style of the Jewish records. It is in harmony with the genealogical, festival-observing, census-taking character of the nation, from the days when Jacob and his seventy descendants went down into Egypt, until the time when the families were numbered on their return from Babylon. The antiquity of all their public days stands or falls with it. There is no place where we can stop and say, here ceases the mythical, the unchronological, and here the chronological commences. From the beginning, from the first intimation of a weekly division of time, from the first mention of a Sabbath, and its subsequent recognition in the heart of the national code, it is all of a piece. Creation is recorded diurnally and chronologically, whether we suppose it to be on the greater or the lesser scale of the world-times. One great earthly use assigned in the appointment of the celestial luminaries is, that "they may be for signs,* and for days, and for years." Besides the general divisions of time produced by the sun and moon, and which were employed, with more or less accuracy, by all nations, the weekly division is acknowledged to have been purely Shemitic in its origin. It is so admitted by Humboldt in his Kosmos. The hebdomadal period, though there are intimations of it in other ancient writings, is found in the Bible as in its native place. The *fact* is accompanied by its *reason*, and both are treated as well known from the beginning. In the event there recorded it had its origin, and as there is nothing astronomical in its character, there could have been no other foundation for such a division than the early knowledge or announcement of the great fact with which the Scriptures connect it.

* Gen. 1 : 14, אֹתֹת, signs—marked periods—epochs.

CHAPTER XIV.

THE ARGUMENT CONTINUED — PROPER NAMES — The Jews a Census-taking People — Their Minute Ritual — The Offerings of the Heads of Tribes, Numbers VII. — The Legal or Documentary Style of the Record — Why this Style, in all Languages, tends to Prolixity — A Solemn Memorial — Wherein it differs from the Style both of Legend and of History — Significance of the Names mentioned, Numbers VII. — Great Number of Proper Names in the Bible — Surpassing those of our Classical Dictionaries — Their Significance a Sign of the National Character — Compared with the Proper Names of the Greek — Both Significant, but in how different a Way! — The one mainly Warlike, the other mainly Religious — Compounded with the Divine Names Jah and El — Include so generally the Ideas of Promise, Covenant and Election — They ever remind the Bearers of the Early Patriarchal Times and the National Seclusion — Named after God — Argument from Numbers VII. — The Religious and Spiritual Character of the Days of the Bondage — Geographical Accuracy — Knowledge on the Spot, Knowledge at the Time.

IN no other people of antiquity, if we except the later Romans, is there anything like that exact census-taking which distinguishes the Jewish chronicles,—that enrolling, not of individuals only, but of ages, and classes, and tribes, and families, and priesthoods, and Levitical services,—those exact inventories of all things required in the ritual and festal worship. Along with this, there is something well calculated to arrest our attention in the proper names of persons, so astonishing in their number and their significance. Has the reader ever thought how many more such names are to be found in this compressed history than in all the poetry and history of classical antiquity! Their strange meanings, too! It is not the mere fact of their having a meaning that is wonderful, for this has been the case more or less among all people; it is the peculiar aspect of their significance, so deeply religious, so intimately and almost universally associated with the divine names and divine things. For an illustration of this census character, as exhibited in almost all the particulars here mentioned, we might take the Seventh chapter of Numbers. Let any one study it carefully as it lies among its contexts, and reconcile it if he can with the theory of its having been made seven hundred years after the professed times, whether as a document entirely new, or as a traditionary compilation. After the long and exceedingly minute accounts of the tabernacle and its furniture, the ark, the altar, the sacrifice, with all the institutions of Jewish worship, we have what may be called the solemn national and tribal inauguration of the whole service. Each head of a tribe, his name given and that of his father, just as we find these same names in their genealogical records elsewhere preserved, brings his representative offering of silver and gold and sacrificial animals, all precisely enumerated, with the measures and values of each. "And the Princes offered for dedicating of the altar in the day that it was anointed, even the Princes offered their offering before the altar. And the Lord said unto Moses, they shall offer their offering, each Prince on his day, for the dedicating of the altar. And he that offered his offering the first day was

Nahshon the son of Amminadab of the tribe of Judah: and his offering was one silver charger, the weight thereof was one hundred and thirty shekels, one silver bowl of seventy shekels, after the shekel of the sanctuary; both of them were full of fine flour mingled with oil for a meat offering: one spoon of ten shekels of gold full of incense; one young bullock, one ram, one lamb of the first year for a burnt offering; one kid of the goats for a sin offering: and for a sacrifice of peace offerings, two oxen, five rams, five he goats, five lambs of the first year: this was the offering of Nahshon the son of Amminadab. On the second day Nethaneel the son of Zuar Prince of Issachar did offer," &c. In this very peculiar document, the very same language, with merely a diversity of the proper names that fill the intervals, is repeated twelve times without abbreviation or any attempt at compression. It might be thought a very tedious paper were it not for the ideas it suggests to the thoughtful reader. It has the diction of a solemn memorial. Viewed in that light there is a reason in the repetition. It is that demand of emphasis which among all nations, ancient or modern, has given an air of prolixity to the law style, as we call it, or documental language. We see something of it in the verbal covenanting of earlier times, as between Abraham and Abimelech, and Abraham and the sons of Heth in the purchase of Macphelah. Here it becomes very striking. Instead of all these precisely similar statements being thrown together with a general caption, or all the later ones referred to the first,—which would have been as clear, one would think, and much more convenient,—each stands separate and full, so that each tribe, and the descendants of each tribe, may see their ancestor's name written out distinctly, with his precise offering, the number, measure, and value, all put down by itself, as though he were the principal name, as he is to them the most interesting name, in all the roll. Now even aside from all this appearance of circumstantiality, no one could regard it as a tradition handed down in memory, or made, wholly or partially, so many centuries after. It would have had, in the one case, the style of legend, in the other, that of history; and both these are different from that of memorial or attestation. If it is impossible to regard it as a forgery, then let one try the other idea of its being a tradition,—so precise a thing coming down with all its names and measures, and its exact order preserved for centuries. If he finds this too hard of belief, then let him take this Seventh of Numbers, and, viewing it as a true memorial, made at the time, let him study it carefully in its connections before and after, and see how much he is compelled to *take with it*,—in other words, how much throughout the Pentateuch must be held as genuine, if this is genuine, how much of all those other books, away back to Genesis, must be taken as a studied preparation, all made to suit, in fact, if this be a forgery,—and then how some of these other passages necessitate still the same thought in respect to others, and so on, throughout these strange writings so fragmentary in some of their appearances and yet found to be, on closer examination, so wondrously coherent. If this document is a reality, made at the time, then is the preparatory work and ritual all a reality, then is that wilderness life a reality, then is that solemn law-giving a reality, Sinai is a reality, and so is the Exodus, and the bondage, for they are all commemorated here or in the closely-connected antecedents; and then Moses is a reality, and Joseph, and the Fathers; then, above all, are the old promises a reality, and the "Covenant" a reality,—for they pervade every part as the meaning and life of the whole. Let the reader think, too, what an immense amount of statistical fact must have been carried down floating in the memory if this were so carried down, and how different that

Jewish memory must have been from the magnifying, coloring, myth-making memory of all other ancient nations. Let any one thus study the passage in connection with these ideas, and he will find, we think, that there is but one conceivable solution of the problem.

We cannot pass over this chapter without dwelling briefly on some striking thoughts presented by its proper names. To set them in their strongest light we give them in the original and with their translations, though of the latter it must be said that we can only be certain of the two fundamental ideas that enter into each name, the manner of connecting them being that about which philologists may differ. Thus *Eliab* has the two ideas, God and father; but we cannot certainly decide whether the significance intended was "*God my Father*," or "*God of my father*." Almost every name in this list has a clear meaning. There is first, of the tribe of

Judah,	נַחְשׁוֹן	Nahshon, Blessed Omen, son of
	עַמִּינָדָב	Amminadab, The Princely :
Issachar,	נְתַנְאֵל	Nethaneel, God hath given, son of
	צוּעָר	Zuar, The Little One, the Lowly :
Zebulon,	אֱלִיאָב	Eliab, God my Father :
Reuben,	אֱלִיצוּר	Elizur, God my Rock, son of
	שְׁדֵיאוּר	Shedeur, the Almighty my Light :
Simeon,	שְׁלֻמִיאֵל	Shelumiel, God my Peace, son of
	צוּרִישַׁדָּי	Zurishaddai, The Almighty my Rock :
Gad,	אֶלְיָסָף	Eliasaph, God will increase, son of
	דְּעוּאֵל	Deuel, Calling on God :
Ephraim	אֱלִישָׁמָע	Elishama, My God will hear, son of
	עַמִּיהוּד	Ammihud, My People,—Glory :

Manasseh,	גַּמְלִיאֵל	Gamliel, God will recompense, son of
	פְּדָהצוּר	Pedahzur, Rock — Redemption :
Asher,	פַּגְעִיאֵל	Pageel, God—Intercession, son of
	עָכְרָן	Okran, Trouble or Sorrow.

What a religious aspect do they possess! Bad men may have godly names ; bad parents may give their children godly names; but their general prevalence does prove that not many generations back there must have been a somewhat generally diffused spirit of piety, or some strongly theistic national ideas, to account for them. So among the Greeks, cowards may have had warlike titles, but the general prevalence of corresponding appellations is very rationally taken as a proof, if there were no other, that the Athenians were a military and naval people. What then is the just inference from the Jewish names as compared with the Greek and Roman?

What is the real historical significance of their deeply religious character, their strong theistic, or rather monotheistic aspect, their continual expression of faith and hope, their so frequent allusions to the ideas of covenant and redemption? The hypothesis of the rationalist utterly fails here; his data are altogether too narrow to account for the strange difference in this apparently so simple a matter of naming. And why too, we may ask, do so many of these appellations end in El and Jah, ever calling up the two great divine names with their most holy ideas? Let the reader ponder well the fact, and see if he can find any other reason for this *national seal*, this naming after the Lord, as we may call it, than the great all-explaining fact that they were, indeed, "a chosen people," an "elect people," whom, for high and world-wide reasons, God had taken *as his own* "when he separated the sons of Adam and gave the nations their inheritance."

The heads of tribes mentioned Numbers

vii., must have been born in the days of the bondage. Now we generally associate with that period the ideas of religious or spiritual decline. They are thought to have been a vile, ungrateful, murmuring people, who had forgotten, or had never known, their ancestral history, and how very religious it was. But here is a little beam of light thrown back upon that dark passage in chronology. In the later days of the bondage they may have become, indeed, debased. Such would be a natural effect of their servile condition. But in the times that followed the death of Joseph, there may have been, there probably was, much religious feeling among them. This style of naming points to such a period. *Jehovah my Light*, the *Redeemer my Rock*, *God the Intercessor*, or He who *intervenes* for relief in the day of trouble,—the *Gift of God*, the *Son of the Lowly*:—Such appellations might have become matters of formality, as is doubtless the case often with names that have come down from a Puritan ancestry, but they had their origin in the spirit and remembrance of the old never to be forgotten promises. There is faith in them somewhere, such faith as Paul sets forth in his long list, Heb. xi., such faith as was counted "to them for righteousness." They are connected, we say, with the divine appellations as seals of the national "covenant," as a standing memorial, handed down from generation to generation, that "this was the people whose God," whose El or Mighty One, "was Jehovah." They came from men who remembered the Preserver of Joseph, who had heard of the visits of Angels, the dream of Bethel, the Hope of Jacob, the Fear of Isaac, the Faith of Abraham, the God of the Covenant, who had been their fathers' God, and who had given them those glorious promises, uneffaceable by the bondage of generations, that in them and their seed all the nations of the earth were to be blessed. Such must have been their source. Or will the "rationalist" rather seek the ground of these ideas, so pure and holy, so full of hope, of simple yet majestic faith, in the monstrous symbolism of old Egypt? Were they seminated in that same Nilotic bed so prolific even then in those physical and spiritual deformities which reached the consummation of all impurity in the unclean worship of Osiris and the dog Anubis?

There is the same peculiarity in the names of places, in the statement of distances and directions. If it be all a compilation, how vast must have been the knowledge of these compilers! The strictest research of modern times, had they enjoyed the benefit, could not have given them an ethnological and geographical accuracy so perfect that the most learned criticism fails to detect a misnomer or an anachronism. It could not be so, unless it were taken from the life. It is knowledge *on the spot*, knowledge at the time, and yet, in some cases, showing such a historical relation, not simply to later, but to the latest times, even to our time, and times beyond it, that it must have been the dual work of an eye-witness writing for the then present, yet guided by a higher mind that looked far down into the remotest future. There is a peculiar clearness in the giving of marked chronological periods, whose importance, though simply Jewish at the time, is now seen to be so closely connected with the general chronology of all history. Thus we have the precise date of the building of Solomon's Temple, and the interval between it and the Exodus! It comes in most naturally, and in strictest keeping with the solemnity of the transaction. Doubtless there had been a most thorough examination, for that purpose, of all known records, and of those tribal and family genealogies in the keeping of which the whole history of the Jews shows them to have been so exact. But this date, though so strictly national, becomes an epoch from which the history of the world looks both back and forward; whilst from its connection with Tyre, and the reign of Hiram, it becomes also one of the noteworthy side points from which we connect the separate and secluded Jewish, with the world's chronology.

CHAPTER XV.

ARGUMENT FROM THE NATURAL CONTINUED — THE BOLDEST OF FORGERIES, OR WHOLLY TRUE — Illustrations from the Prophets — Isaiah's Vision, "in the year that King Uzziah died" — Naturalness of this Mnemonic Date — Why the Prophet should remember it — Peculiar History of Uzziah, the Leper King — Dates of the Prophetic Visions — The Day, the Month, and the Year — Jeremiah and Ezekiel. Argument from these Facts — The Wholesale Forgery easier of Belief than this minute Filling up — Would betray a Consciousness of Falsehood inconsistent with any subjective Truthfulness — Driven to the First Hypothesis — Comparison with Homer — The Homeric Truthfulness — Why does it not also prove the Homeric Supernatural — Difference between the Homeric and the Bible Supernatural — Parallel between the Greeks and Jews — What necessary to make it complete — The Greek Zeus and the Hebrew Jehovah — The Greek Idea of Fate, and the Jewish Ideas of Covenant and Election — The Greek Oracles, the Hebrew Messiah — The Hebrews a World-nation, The Greeks had no World-idea.

FURTHER illustrations of this statistical character we find in the reigns of the Kings, and in the dates of remarkable events as referred to some striking time or fact in those reigns; the truthful impression being, in most cases, made stronger by the informal and incidental manner of their introduction. In dry history this style of reference, or incidental date-giving, would not so much surprise us; but we meet with it in the very visions of the Prophets. "In the year that King Uzziah died," says Isaiah, "I saw the Lord sitting upon a throne high and lifted up, and his train filled the temple. Above it stood the seraphim, and they cried, one to the other, saying Holy, Holy, Holy, is the Lord of Hosts, the whole earth is full of his glory." Let any one have his mind impressed as it ought to be impressed with this seraphic glory; let him think of the high state of soul necessary even for the conception of such a vision with its air of ineffable holiness, and then, if he can, connect it, and its inseparable associations, with that meanest of all falsehood, the petty circumstantial lie. But take away this revolting thought (though necessary to the idea of a mere filled up compilation) and every thing lies before us in grand consistency. The date mentioned is the last one that would have been selected by a forger, or guessed by a compiler, to give a mnemonic importance to any incident; but to Isaiah himself it had a mournful interest. "It was in the year that King Uzziah died,"—that old leper-stricken king, who had so long "lived in a separate house," where, "free among the dead," he had poured forth his sorrows in that mournful 88th Psalm so strikingly descriptive of his sad condition.([8]) His passing away, at last, would be a much more eventful remembrance to the Prophet than to the nation at large; for he had long been civilly dead. During the latter part of his long reign of fifty and two years, he was entirely cut off from public business, and "Jotham his son was Regent over the king's house, judging the people of the land." The superseded father must have been nearly forgotten by the multitude, and his death and hasty unroyal burial could have made but little impression upon their minds. But Isaiah had been his counsellor, sometimes his reprover;

he had written the history of his earlier active life. He had thought much of the old monarch,—of his better days, when "he sought the Lord and God made him to prosper,"—of his more peaceful days, "when he digged wells, and had cattle in the low country, and vine-dressers upon the mountains, for he loved husbandry,"—of his grand, warlike days, when "he fought with the Philistines, and brake down the wall of Gath, and strengthened Jerusalem with towers, and smote the Arabians that dwelt in Gur-baal, and built Eloth, and spread his name and power even to the entering in of Egypt." He had often pictured, if he could not visit, him in his lone leper-house; he called to mind that offence against the divine *ceremonial* holiness for which he had been smitten with unapproachable impurity; and it was in the year so well remembered from all these sad and humbling associations, the year when this old forgotten monarch "slept," at last, "with his fathers," that Isaiah had that vision of *ineffable* holiness, too bright for impure eyes to see, for "unclean lips to tell." The vision is a reality; that is, the Prophet did see the Throne, the Glory, and the burning Seraphim, whether it were from a divine afflatus or his own inward rapt enthusiasm. We are not afraid thus to state the case, because deeply convinced that one who can thus receive fully the *subjective*, will find himself unable to resist the belief of the *absolute* truthfulness. The vision is a reality; the Prophet is a reality, and then the dying king is a reality; Uzziah's reign is a reality, and then that which made it what it was, even the reign of "Amaziah his father, whose mother's name was Jehoaddan of Jerusalem," that, too, was a reality, and the reign before it was a reality, and so on. For there is no place where we can stop, until we find the consistency of all subsequent Jewish history, the seminal elements of its strength and weakness, in the reigns of David and Saul, and the events of those times all prepared by the events before them, and so on, until we come up to the recorded life of him who first wrote in his book, or received from older books, that "in the beginning God created the Heavens and the earth."

And so is it with the Prophets throughout. They keep a diary of their visions, and if it is false, it is far more false, more incredibly false, than either their rapt subjective states or their wild harangues. Jeremiah and Ezekiel manifest this trait more strikingly than Isaiah. Everywhere do these seers record the dates, the year, the month, the day of the month, the attending chronological circumstances of the burthens and messages with which as they allege they have been commissioned by the Lord. If these dates are put in by themselves, then is it all, subjectively, one harmonious consistent picture of life. If supposed to be put in by compilers, long after the times of the prophetic visions, then there is no reason for it, no meaning in it. It is not only incredible but absurd. It destroys its own credit, and the credit of that which it would attest. It is an easier theory that every word of the Prophetic writings had been forged. If that is *incredible*, then this is most *incredible*. There is but one other supposition: the dates and the visions are from the same persons, and these are the prophets themselves writing and speaking at the times they profess to write and speak, and in relation to actual existing events that form the subjects of their warning. The seers, the times, the nation, the national life, it is all one true picture,—*in its parts*, most truthful and natural, *in its whole*, suggestive of an extraordinary and difficult problem. Let any man attempt to explain its natural without bringing in its supernatural, or some other supernatural—if he can.

Either of these suppositions, except the first, tries our credulity to its utmost strain. To suppose that this amount of statistical statement, from Seth to Malachi, all came from tradition alone, and was carried down by tradition, or was ever assumed to have been so carried, or that all these numbers, round and mixed, these dates, these minute coïncidences of events, this immense body of proper names, surpassing, we think, all that are to be found in classical dictionaries, these countless genealogies, were all carried in the popular or the individual memory until the later times of the Jewish history,—this is beyond all belief. Equally incredible, more incredible, we think, that they should have been put in by late compilers as the arbitrary or conjectural filling up of outline historical events traditionally received.

The wholesale forgery is the easier of belief, the forgery in which the great facts as well as the minutest statistics are all supposed to be mere creations of the imagination. There is, too, less wrong to conscience. A man must feel less guilty in producing a whole and continuous work of fiction, than in thus tampering with, and perverting, what is supposed to be true ; if it can be supposed to be true by one who could thus deliberately deal with it. There must be felt to be in this circumstantial falsehood, thus thrust into a traditionary outline, a crime and a meanness that does not attach to the bolder work. Hence, viewing it as myths, or detached national stories thus falsely filled up, we cannot have even as much respect for the Jewish history as for the early Greek so truthfully left in its natural cloudiness, its wild legendary state, without any attempt to give it a minuteness of detail it could not naturally and truly possess. The bolder forgery, we say again, has the less difficulty. The view of Paine, and of others like him, though it be called crude and unlearned, though it be stigmatized as "vulgar infidelity," is really easier than some theories that have been entertained by the Straussian and Westminster schools. It is easier to believe in the making an entire new temple, incredible as that may seem when we think what a temple it is, than in the filling up an old tumbling ruin with such elaborately-wrought cornices and carved work, to say nothing of Cherubim and Seraphim, and holy symbolism, so utterly out of place unless regarded as representative of ideas that must have constituted the ground and reason of the whole structure.

And now, if such wholesale forgery, as we first showed, is really beyond all belief, then there remains but one conclusion. The first of our three suppositions is the only solution of the difficulty. *The whole Jewish history is true,*—as true in its details, its dates, its numbers—making all allowance for human injuries in transcription—as in its general outlines. The evidence for the one part cannot be taken out, without rending away all foundation for belief in the other. But take it all away, and there is no possible means of solving the greatest problem that history presents,—namely, the influence of this imagined nation, this ideal religion, upon the whole course of human affairs and human thinking. Receive it as a whole, and it has a strange supernatural light, a world-light, that we receive along with it. It explains itself and vastly more in history besides. Take it in any other way, it not only leaves us in darkness, but becomes itself the most inexplicable problem ever presented to the human mind.

The only writer in all antiquity who makes any approach to this Bible finish, though still at a vast distance from it, is Homer ; and this is the very reason why we are so impressed with the truthfulness of his descriptions of life. In his catalogue of the Grecian ships and armies, (although in the main employing round numbers,) in his accurate geography, in his graphic local touches, in his family stories, he presents a picture, whose falsehood it is difficult to conceive. We do not hesitate to say it—we believe in Homer,—and no common effort of sceptical literary dissertation would make us yield the faith. We have more trust in many of the scenes of the Odyssey than in the relations of some modern travellers. His wild and fanciful supernatural sits loose from his descriptive narrative. It is not so religiously and morally interwoven as in the Bible histories. It is, therefore, quite easy to separate it, and when we do so, the thoughtful reader who can enter into the Homeric spirit, cannot help feeling that in other respects, the Iliad and the Odyssey are among the most truthful of books. If it were not so, no amount of the mere marvellous would ever have given them such a lasting place in the heart of the world.

But why not, then, take his supernatural too, on the grounds of the argument we are now using in respect to the Bible? The answer is easy, and we think conclusive. There is first, that immense and essential difference between the two supernaturals on which we have previously insisted. Every candid, thoughtful mind, certainly every truly religious mind, must see and acknowledge it. The Jehovah of the Scriptures, and the Zeus of Homer! the angel visits of the Old Testament, and the Homeric deities sinking below the human in the part they take in the strifes of men! the divine guardianship of a chosen nation, as preparatory to a chosen church to be gathered from all nations, and the petty providence of the god of Ida which, though extending much beyond the blind selfish passions of the other powers, is yet so limited by the Trojan and Grecian camp! let go the mere scenery and take alone the moral conceptions; bring them fairly before the mind and we need say no more. But why is the supernatural of the Bible so different from that of other ancient nations, so greatly different, that in the absence of other reasons, and no others can be found, it can only be explained on the ground of the supernatural itself? The whole case might here be rested, but the question may demand, and we are willing to give, a wider answer. We say then, to make the cases wholly parallel, had there been connected with the Homeric stories throughout, had there preceded and followed them in Grecian history, a supernatural like that of the Bible, possessing every where the same high moral reason and the same religious dignity, we should have been compelled to receive it on the same ground. But to fill out the parallelism to its widest extent, we must make a supposition long in time and corresponding to the whole collateral field. We say again then—Had there been, not only in Homer, who gleams upon us like a light in the desert, but in a series of Hellenic writers before and after him, the same ever consistent mingling of their earthly history with a high superhuman providence, and an eventful human destiny ever held forth as the religious ground of the national life,—had there been a Father of the Faithful, like Abraham, among the *γηγενεις* or old ancestral stock of the Athenians, had the days of the Sons of Hellen presented something like the Patriarchal life with its pure trust in the One most high God, had some grand pyramidal figure like Moses towered up amid those chaotic myths of the Dorians and Ionians, had there been a Noah among the old Pelasgi, or some traditions of an Enoch who "walked with God" and was taken away from a sin-deluged world,—had there been in the early Grecian "mythical" something like the visits of angels to rest-seeking, world-weary pilgrims, and divine appearances for righteous retribution instead of the fanciful, unmeaning apotheoses of a Bacchus or a Hercules,—had "the sons of Javan and Elisha and Kittim and Dodanim" brought with them from the East, and ever preserved among their descendants, such a holy genealogical record as has been carried down by their early consanguinei the Sons of Eber,—had this ancient document thus preserved by them furnished the only key to a universal ethnology, or assumed to do so,—above all, had there come out of these

Javanic or Ionic roots (for they are the same original word) such a nation as the Israelites with their wonderful monotheism and their most religious law, carrying down with them in their earliest records, and as repeated continually in their later writings, such catholic promises that "in them all the nations of the earth should be blessed,"—had there been ever prominent in Grecian thought, instead of *fate* and *destiny*, the ideas of covenant and election,—had there been all along in place of Dodonean triflings and petty Delphic cheats, a grand series of Messianic oracles, commencing with one older than Prometheus, and holding forth the "Desire of all nations," not merely as an artistic or scientific civilizer, but as the long-expected spiritual deliverer of our sin-burdened humanity,—had these Messianic oracles kept growing clearer and clearer, pointing more and more to the unearthly and the heavenly, until there had at last arisen in this favored Hellas, this land of "the covenant," some one so human yet so superhuman as to be justly claimed as their fulfiller, and in whom might have been discovered a resemblance, not to Pythagoras, or Plato, or to Socrates even, but to Jesus of Nazareth,—could we thus fill up the parallel (and who can take exception to the mode of doing it) then would we be prepared to answer the question fully, we think, satisfactorily, conclusively. Had the supernatural of Homer and the Greek logographers been of this kind, had it been grounded on such a "covenant," supported by such promises so anciently uttered and for all humanity,—had it contained such world-oracles, and had the great series of events connected with them terminated in the advent of such a Messiah, then could we have believed in a Grecian supernatural, and regarded the Sons of Javan, or the Hellenic race, as "Chosen of God," the "Elect of God," the First Born among the nations, as the race called out from the common heathenism, supernaturally ruled of heaven, destined to be a light to the barbarians and to all people who sat in the darkness of idolatry and sin.

CHAPTER XVI.

THE NATURAL IN THE HISTORY OF CHRIST — The Birth of Christ — The Visit of the Magi — The Legendary Aspect has come from the Romish Traditions — How Different the Bible would have been had it been compiled in a Later Age — Saint Stories, The Talmud — The Universal Eastern Belief in the Coming of a Hero Messiah, or El Gibbor — The Angels and the Shepherds — No Human Invention these — Sublimity of the Announcement — "Glory to God in the Highest; on Earth Peace, Good Will to Men" — The Temptation — Its Truthfulness, Subjective and Objective — The Crucifixion — "Then sitting down they watched him there." — Holiness and Suffering unsurpassed — How strange if there had been no Outward Witnessing of Nature — This Human, this Natural, the Whole of it! — Incredible — God Beholding yet Indifferent! — Still more Incredible — Beholding with Interest, yet that Interest never manifested, never to be manifested! — This surpasses all belief — A Divine Interest immeasurable in its Intensity — The Incredible of the Sense as opposed to the Credibility of the Higher Thinking—or the Incredibility of the Reason.

ON the supernatural in the history of Christ we have already partially dwelt. Take out all the directly miraculous, and there is nothing on earth so human. Nowhere, too, does this show itself more strongly than in the midst of the most astoundingly marvellous that accompanied his birth and crucifixion. Where every thing would have tempted to the wonder-making style, it is there precisely that we have all that is most sober in the manner of the narration, most truthful and probable in the connection with it of the antecedent and surrounding events of history. The story of the Magi, and especially, as some would regard it, the oriental style of its commencement, might seem an exception to this. "Now when Jesus was born in Bethlehem of Judea in the days of Herod the King, lo, there came wise men from the east to Jerusalem." It does appear, at first view, to have a little of the legendary look; but when we examine carefully the source of such a feeling, it is found to have come from the legends that the Church of Rome has made out of it, and which we associate, in style if not in fact, with the original picture. In the same way has there been given to the passages that speak of the Virgin a coloring of thought different from what they would otherwise have possessed. There is, however, an important view of Bible truth to be learned from this. We see from these Romish legends what the New Testament would have been, or rather what a different aspect would have been given to its narrations, had its early materials been left floating until they had been gathered into a written form by these traditionists. How very different from the plain histories of Matthew, Mark, Luke and John, would have been our Gospels, had they been first compiled in the Fifth or Sixth century! There might not, perhaps, have been more of the miraculous, but it would have had another style; it would have been the predominant thing, and by its swelling features have betrayed this false position. The actual presence of the superhuman, or its close proximity, made the spirit sober; the deep conviction of the evangelical writers, so different from the inflating legendary faith, kept down the tendency to the mere wonder-feeling and wonder-making. These are aspects of style inseparable from narrations of the supernatural made long after the miraculous epoch has passed away. They betray the fact that the reality to which they refer is removed to a great distance. They show effort, perhaps unconscious effort, to make up for this distance, and the loss of the near impression, by disproportion and exaggeration. Thus we see, too, what the truthful histories of the Old Testament would have become under a similar process in the hands of the later Rabbins. The Talmud and the Romish saint-stories are proof enough of the kind of shape the whole Bible would have taken, had not superhuman power intervened continually for the preservation of its human truthfulness.

For the reasons given, this story of the "Wise men from the East" has at first something of the legendary aspect, and yet, when we come to view it in all its connections, there is no event that fits more exactly, not only with the Jewish, but with the consistency, and most sober aspect, of the world's general history. We are assured by a Roman author well acquainted with the fact about which he writes, that at this time there prevailed, throughout the East, an opinion that some great one was about to arise who should possess the dominion of the world, and that Judea was the country in which his birth was to be expected—"percrebuerat Oriente toto *vetus* et constans opinio, *esse in fatis*, ut eo tempore Judea profecti rerum potirentur." This vetus opinio, or ancient belief, was but the expansion of the great Messianic idea of the Hebrew Prophets, or of the still older idea that had come from the earliest times, even from the days of that primitive patriarchal revelation of which every Eastern nation had preserved some remains. In the Book of Job we have evidence that it was not confined to the Jews. The visions of Balaam show that it was common to the earliest seers, and had place among "the Children of the East." Aside from direct history, aside from the Messianic oracles whether of the Jews or of other nations, aside from the Messianic tradition as more or less appearing in the distortions of all the Eastern religions,—aside from all this, what more natural and probable than the idea itself, even if we suppose it to have arisen spontaneously, without oracle or special revelation, in the human mind! What more consistent with the highest truthfulness of human conceptions, than this thought of a Saviour, a Redeemer, a hero, a mighty one, who should come in the latter day for the deliverance of our sin-wearied humanity! This feeling would reach its crisis when the whole political power of the world was seen gathering to one head. No wonder that the more secular and ambitious minds interpreted the old wide-spread oracle of the Roman emperor. The more thoughtful souls looked in a different direction. Many things would turn them to the land of Judea. The Israelitish nation had become, from various reasons, an object of special attention. They had begun to make a conspicuous chapter in Roman history. Their captivity in Babylon and Persia had left remembrances such as had accompanied no other nations conquered by those strong empires. Wherever they were known, and they were now beginning to be known quite widely, they were recognized as a "peculiar," a very "peculiar people." There was at this time a Jewish school in Babylon, which was among the chief controllers of thought in the East. Isaiah shows a knowledge of the Persian ([9]) doctrine of Good and Evil, and nothing is more probable than that the followers of Zoroaster, or the Magi, or "Wise Men," as they are called in the gospel, should have had some knowledge of his glowing prophecies respecting the wondrous child to be born of a virgin, and who was to be called The "El Gibbor," the "Mighty One," the "Prince of Peace." Under such a thought, too, the pilgrimage undertaken was an event in perfect keeping with the thinking and feeling of those countries and those times.

Turn we now to a different scene, in harmony with, and yet presenting a most impressive contrast to, the one we have already been contemplating. This world-wide story of a Messiah to be born was not only the study of the Eastern sage, but formed the topic of nightly conversation among the shepherds in "the hill country of Judea." "And there were in the same country shepherds abiding in the field, keeping watch over their flocks by night. And lo, the angel of the Lord came upon them, and the glory of the Lord shone round about them; and they were sore afraid. And the angel said unto them, Fear not; for behold, I bring you glad tidings of great joy which shall be to all people. For unto you is born this day in the city of David, a Saviour which is Christ the Lord. And this shall be to you the sign; ye shall find the babe wrapped in swaddling clothes, lying in a manger. And suddenly there was with the angel a multitude of the Heavenly host praising God and saying—*Glory to God in the highest, and on earth peace, good will* (10) *towards men.*" No human faculty of invention ever invented this; no human imagination ever filled it up, or magnified it from some rudimentary fact or scene. We feel that the picture is perfect; to touch is to deface it. It is unique in itself; it never had additions or alterations; it never grew. The scene is one total impression. There is no one part we can select as the germ of the rest. There were shepherds watching their flocks by night, and discoursing with each other about certain strange rumors that then filled the whole "hill country of Judea." They had heard the story of Zachariah. They knew the universal expectation in regard to the Son of David, and the universal feeling that his advent was near at hand. Their views of Him may have been very erroneous, but their hearts were full of the expected glory.

Is it strange that they saw a light in the heavens? Call it fancy if you will, an excited imagination; we are only arguing here for the subjective truthfulness of the narration. Is it strange that they heard voices in the air around them and above them? Say if you will that their awed feelings, and their wondrously elated hopes, shaped these sounds into the glorious words that are recorded. Here is the great, the real wonder. It is the spiritual marvel that throws in the background the physical strangeness. We believe in the miracle on the ground of the doctrine conveyed; we find it easy to give credence to an outward supernatural as attested by the sublimity of such a message. It is nothing so strange that shepherds should see lights in the heaven, that they should hear voices in the air; but such voices, such words, arranged in such a sentence, that has not yet ceased, and never will cease, to vibrate through the heart of humanity—"Behold, I bring you glad tidings of great joy which shall be to all people,—Glory to God in the highest; on earth peace, good will toward men." We leave out of the account the idea of sheer forgery as something too incredible for any sane mind to entertain. A light *was* seen; sounds were heard, whether by the ear of the sense, or the ear of the imagination, or the ear of the most truthful inner spirit. The scene thus far was a reality, the light was a reality, the voices a reality! If wholly subjective, it is only the more wonderful reality. What was there in the common thought of these shepherds, in their culture, their associations of ideas, that should have so shaped the vision, and brought out upon the airy undulations that sublimest collocation of words the world had ever heard, that message of divine peace so far beyond what philosophy had ever conceived, or poetry had ever dreamed. It drives us to the outward supernatural as the easier explanation of the mystery: Why should there not have been a light from heaven, and a voice from heaven, when such a truth was uttered? If convinced that it is subjectively true, then, for the mind that truly conceives the scene and the idea, it is difficult to withhold assent from the full reality, in the widest sense of that Protean word. We have ever been led to regard this narration in Luke as one of the key passages of the Scriptures, or one of those infallible proof texts where the divine beauty and glory so shine out that we cannot easily conceive of falsehood. Heaven is here come down to earth; it lies all around us;—how pure the air, how clear the light, how holy the revelation! Glory to God in the highest; on earth peace, good will to men. If this is unreal, what then on this poor earth of ours can be regarded as real? There is a power in truthful representation, when we can conceive it aright, that is irresistible. We know it as we know the sun that shines, the heat that warms, the emotion that we feel, the very thought we are thinking. And thus there is a conviction that enables us to say with boldness, if this passage in Luke is an unreality, then is our whole life an unreality; philosophy, and science, and history, and theology, and all opinions, and all religions, are but the veriest dreams of a visionary, unsubstantial existence.

In the same manner, too, may we separate the subjective from the objective truthfulness in the history of "the temptation;" and this not for the purpose of denying or undervaluing, but of confirming the outward narrative. The Child of such a birth, so strange and said to be so strangely heralded,—we cannot wonder that from his youth he should have been filled with the idea of a divine mission, and that even at the tender age of twelve years he should have felt that "he must be about his Father's business." Then, too, does it cease to be strange that he, as well as those he came to deliver, must have a struggle with the Great Power of evil. This admitted, the fasting, the wilderness life, are all truthful for such a character, all, too, in strict accordance with the ascetic ideas of those who were esteemed most pious, most unearthly in that age. "And when he was an hungered the devil came unto him." Say, if you please, that it was a vision occasioned by his abnormal physical state. It may have been none the less real, none the less designed by God as the very means for its production. But the inward conflict—the soul strife—how truthful the representation of that war in the spirit, how grand the lesson that he who saves us from sin and temptation had himself to go through the process by which he was to know, not *a priori*, from known or conceived causes, or *a posteriori*, from seen effects, but *in se*, *in præsenti*, from actual personal experience, what temptation is, and how the soul *feels* when assailed by it. Such a High Priest became us who was tempted in all respects, κατὰ πάντα καθ᾽ ὁμοιότητα, as we are tempted, yet without sin. This is the essential reality; and when this is conceived as it ought to be, how easy to believe the less reality of a true personal objective presence as the accompaniment and representative of so mighty and real a power! The writer thinks he cannot be misinterpreted in the views here given. He does not deny the objective; he holds to the objective; but he would wish to present strongly the greater wonder of the natural and human working, as that which makes not barely credible only, but easy of belief, the supernatural and superhuman accompaniment. Let one believe in the perfect truthfulness of the Magi visit, the shepherds' annunciation, the spiritual struggle with the tempting power, and then, the moving meteor, the celestial glory, the demon appearance, the angelic voices, become, at once, expected and harmonious accompaniments of the higher reality. If one does not thus believe in the human, if he does not know enough of the human,—his own human, or the human in general,—to make such conceptions possible to him, and to give them the high air of reality, then would all supernatural manifestations be in vain. "He would not believe truly, though one rose from the dead.' He would not believe because there is for him nothing in the credible of the reason, of the conscience, or the spiritual discernment, to carry him against the incredibility of the sense.

There is no page in the Bible more intensely human than that which records the crucifixion of Christ, and yet there is no one that so directly draws the mind to the thought of the unearthly and the supernatural. The malice of the Priests, the cruelty of the fickle multitude, the wrath of the national prejudices, the Roman "caring for none of these things,"—Caiphas, Pilate, Pilate's wife, the soldiers, the frightened disciples, the clamoring mob,—how human are they all! The sufferer, too, in their midst,—keep out of view all higher thoughts, and where was a more perfect manhood ever exhibited to the world! How different from the humanity around him, and yet how truly man! Take up the book and read. Does a shade of scepticism cross the Christian mind, we know of no better prescription for such a disease than this: Take up the book and read the story of the crucifixion. There is no need of retouching the picture. Nothing can add to the divine limning of the scene as presented in the Evangelists. Thus far, we venture to say, no sane mind can have any more doubt of its reality than of any event of yesterday narrated by the most authentic of human testimony. Thus far there is nothing in Thucydides or Tacitus, nothing in Robertson or Prescott, nothing in any book of Memoirs, nothing in any Biography, ancient or modern, to be compared with it. We feel throughout the power of a graphic truthfulness that is wholly irresistible. But there is one point in which it seems to be all condensed. It is the close of the drama so far as the mere human agency is concerned. The soldiers' more active work is done. With stolid indifference have they nailed him to the cross, then raised it high in air. "They parted his garments among them;" and then, says the author of this inimitable narrative, "then sitting down they watched him there." It was with no feeling of compassion. All that they had now to do was to await with military patience that lingering agony they so well knew, and to which they had become so indifferent. The beginning of the work is put for the consummation. "They crucified him," says the Evangelist; "then sitting down they watched him there."

Here is the end of the human, the natural. So far all is credible, probable, irresistibly truthful. But can the mind rest here? Will it not become incredible again if there is nothing more? The series of events culminates in this one scene presented to their eyes, now presented to our imaginations. What have we before us? A holy and innocent being, the most holy the world had ever known, made to suffer the most lingering and agonizing pain. Now turn we from the credible of sense and nature to the higher credible, the higher truthfulness demanded by the moral reason and the conscience. Here is the spectacle;—and now we ask, Which is the greater wonder,—that this should be the whole of it, all finished here on earth, with nothing more in any world beyond, in any heaven above or hell below, in any time then present, in any time to come,—that this should continue to be the whole of it, this natural, this human merely, or that there should be some manifestation from a higher sphere in attestation of some higher ideas than those that filled the minds of revengeful Jews, or the watching Roman soldiers? The bare sight, the bare conception of the outward scene, has of itself a strangeness, an *a priori* incredibility which even the familiarity of sense cannot wholly take away. A holy soul thus suffering! But add another thought. Thus suffering all alone, no higher soul beholding! How the wonder rises! Beholding, yet indifferent! It passes all belief. Beholding with interest, with interest most intense—for no movement of the Divine soul can be either small or measurable—and yet that interest never, never manifested, and never to be manifested *in any outward sign.* We have reached the utmost climax of the marvellous. But granting it to be conceivable, still the question returns : Is this the *less* wonder, or that the earth should quake, the rocks should rend, and darkness cover all the land, when the Omnipotent Holiness is thus defied, and the proof is challenged, as it were, that the higher world is not, and cannot be, indifferent to such a spectacle? We cannot bear the thought, when we think and feel aright. No miraculous in nature can surpass it in incredibility. There is mind somewhere, some higher mind, some universal soul, to whom such a scene is matter of intensest interest; and just as strongly do we feel that this interest must display itself. The publicity of right, the manifestation of right, is just as much a demand of the reason as the absolute existence of right. It must become objective, or the essential idea is marred. At some time, in some way, will it so come out, that not only will the reason acknowledge it to be a truth, but the eye shall see, the ear shall hear, the inmost sense shall feel it as the deepest fact, the highest reality, of the universe. It may not be now, nor nigh, yet such objective manifestation will surely be. Even in ordinary cases of wrong we cannot keep out the thought. Things will not pass away, the universe will not go on its eternal course with any wrong, the least wrong, buried in eternal indifference, or forever hidden subjectively in the mind of God, or having its retribution only faintly signalled in some obscure and hard to be interpreted arrangements of unvaried physical law. No soul is ever really satisfied with the common babble about the retribution of nature. The reason, too, has its law, and this demands the supernatural manifestation. Before the world ends, before even nature ends, there must come some higher and more distinct sign, some unmistakable showing that the least moral evil is of more moment than any order, or any disorder, of the material universe.

Thus are we compelled to think even in respect to common wrongs. Here ordinary experience seems to be against what would otherwise be the decision of the reason · and so, "if the vision tarry we wait for it,"—the higher, though for the present overruled, faculty of the soul gathering from the very delay accumulated argument for the great final manifestation. But in such a case as this of the crucifixion, we feel that the scale of credibility turns the other way. The present becomes more easy of belief than the suspended manifestation. The supernatural surprises our sense ; it is opposed to the associations of the lower though the more common experience, and this, its lower incredibility, is the ground of Hume's vulgar argument against miracles. On the other hand, the entire absence of any such manifestation in such a case as this, gives a shock to the higher thinking. It is a higher incredibility that Hume and Bentham were utterly incapable of estimating. Such absence would be a wonder we might receive with a submissive faith, humbly trusting to the revelation of some distant day; still in itself, and to a right mind, would it be a higher marvel, requiring a higher exercise of this faith than is demanded for crediting any of the wonders in nature recorded by the Evangelists.

CHAPTER XVII.

THE MYSTERIOUS CHASM IN CHURCH HISTORY — The Burial of Christ — The Appearance to Mary — At the Sea of Galilee — Subjective Truthfulness of the Stories of the Resurrection — Commencement of the Historical Chasm — "The Acts of the Apostles" — Its Scanty Records — How Little we know of the Apostolic Age! — The New Life in the World — Had come from the Grave of Christ — The Historical Silence like the Chasms discovered in Nature's Progress — The Silent Supernatural coming between the Old and the New Creations — Separates the Inspired from the other Writings of the Church — The Light seen again towards the days of the Apostolical Fathers — A new Power had worked mightily between — Whence came it? — The Apostles carried with them something more than Truth — Beside the Doctrine, they had with them the Risen Life itself of the Crucified — The Phrase ἐν Χριστῷ — Χριστὸς ἐν ὑμῖν — Early Christians styled *Christophori*, Christ-bearers — Justyn Martyr — The Language means more than Discipleship — Unknown to the World before — A new Thought demanded new Words — Favorite Language of Paul — "The New Man" — "The Man in Christ" — Christ in the Church — We study Christ in Paul — Comes nearer to us than in the Evangelists.

"HE was crucified, dead and buried." Here ends the natural, or as we have styled it, the ordinarily credible, in the history of Christ. "When Jesus, therefore, had received the vinegar he said, It is finished; and he bowed his head and gave up the ghost." The soldier had pierced his side to ascertain the fact that he was unmistakably dead. "He who saw it had borne witness" in his own loving and mourning memory to the never to be forgotten event. The rich friend of Arimathea had begged the body of Pilate and taken it down from the cross. The honorable friend Nicodemus, desponding but no longer afraid, had brought "his aromatic mixture of myrrh and aloes about an hundred pounds weight." "Then took they the body of Jesus, and wound it in linen cloths, with the spices, as the manner of the Jews is to bury. Now in the place where he was crucified there was a garden, and in the garden a new sepulchre wherein was never man laid. There laid they Jesus, therefore, because of the Jews' preparation-day; for the sepulchre was nigh at hand." Who can doubt this? What motive to doubt it? What reason to doubt it that would not involve in scepticism every narration of a death and burial ever given to the world? As well doubt that Socrates drank the poisoned cup, or that Washington was entombed at Mount Vernon.

Here ends the scene, we say, in its natural or earthly aspect. Most grave is it, most solemnly impressive, yet within the limits of the ordinary or sense credibility. Certain events are recorded as transpiring afterwards, but they belong to the unearthly or supernatural chapter. It is a part of our present argument to pass them by, though without at all losing sight of them. They are, indeed, supernatural, as viewed in their absolute verity, but it is sufficient, at present, to advert to the subjective truthfulness of the narrative. There is the story of a reäppearance upon earth, of the body being strangely missing from the sepulchre, of the wonder of the disciples when this startling rumor is brought to their desponding minds. One saw the empty grave, and believed that its tenant had risen from the dead. The others, as is evidently implied, went away again to their own homes, still desponding, still unbelieving, "for they knew not the Scriptures,"—they knew not the glory of that new kingdom, of that new life for the world, which, as we now know, beyond all doubting, did truly arise out of that garden sepulchre. The narrative tells of one who had a stronger faith, even that faith whose energy and vitality is love. It was "the woman, the sinner," who "loved much because she had been forgiven much." It might have been this faith stripped even of hope, and reduced to its rudimental element of holy affection,—it might have been this faith, outwardly desponding, yet inwardly still alive, that caused her to see and hear what others saw and heard not. And so might the sceptical objector maintain that it was her own loving fancy that through the dim grey mists of the morning gave shape to the ever-remembered One who had once so tenderly pronounced her sins forgiven. It was her own loving fancy that gave this shadowy form the well-known voice, when it "said unto her, Mary, and she turned herself and said unto him, Rabboni, which is to say, Master." There is a ghostly, imaginative air about it, the critic may say, and with some plausibility ; but who can deny the heavenly strain of the message that follows this brief and touching allocution ? She had started to grasp the body, or the figure, call it what we will, when Jesus saith unto her, " Touch me not, Mary, for I am not yet ascended to my Father ; but go to my brethren, and say unto them, I ascend unto my Father and your Father, and to my God and your God." Fraud here is out of the question ; no soul that has not utterly lost all feeling of the pure and truthful can entertain such a thought for a moment. Fancy may have raised the form, but could any supposed fancy have created such a voice and such a declaration ? Granting, however, that such a solution might seem probable if we had to judge of the story alone, without regard to its antecedents or its consequents, yet, in view of these, now so clear and so well established, how greatly increased the gravity, how essentially changed the whole aspect, of the testimony! We do now know that there has been, for eighteen hundred years, coming forth from that grave a power most unearthly, most superhuman ; a power that none but the most ignorantly obstinate can doubt ; a power that has changed, and is still changing, the face of the world. It is this fact, this knowledge, which may well be regarded as rendering, for us at least, such an objective declaration at the time one of the most credible events that ever happened in human history. The incredibility of the sense and the imagination is lost, yea, overcome an hundred fold, in the higher credibility of the reason, in view of the accompanying truth, and the superhuman historical effect.

And so of the other appearances—the

coming into the midst of the watchful company "when the doors were shut for fear of the Jews," the familiar voice so readily distinguished from its well-known salutation, "Peace be unto you," the "burning hearts" that felt a friend was nigh, though "the eye was holden" from recognizing the changed form that so mysteriously travelled with them from Emmaus to Jerusalem; the sudden clearing up of all that seemed dim and phantom-like as they witnessed the familiar yet solemn act of breaking bread. There is the same feeling as we read the account of that early morning visit at the Sea of Galilee, when again the disciples knew him not until the beloved one recognized the Master's speech in the tender question, "Children, have ye any meat?" "Then were the disciples glad when they saw the Lord." Is this the language, this the style of narration, of wonder-makers or legendary mythopœists? Call it imagination if you will—it may be confessed that there were some grounds for its excitement—but how pure the imagination, how heavenly! If it were subjective merely, how holy that subjectiveness! how calmly restrained by some most unusual, if not unearthly influence! What can be more truthful than the manner of narration, and what more incredible than that it should have been so told by men who knew that it was all a lying picture, whose most minute and tender touches would, on such a supposition, be the grossest of all mendacities? To think of *such* a story, and *so* told, by men who had stolen their Master's lifeless body, and knew that it was lying concealed somewhere, a decomposing corpse! To think of such truthful simplicity, such enthusiasm, such earnestness, such courage, such elevated thought, such holy emotion, such a heavenly life of love, such martyr deaths coming from such a source!—of so much unearthly vitality, in short, proceeding from a mouldering death, so much spiritual splendor from the darkness of a hopeless grave; so much heavenly truth, or truth that seems so heavenly, from known lies, so revolting to any pure conscience, so alien to all elevated hope, so inconsistent with any moral heroism, so utterly destructive of any martyr spirit, of any soul-sustaining faith! Incredible, most incredible! Almost any miracle is more worthy of belief; while, in contrast with it, the holy, the consistent, the harmonious supernatural of Christ's real objective resurrection becomes the most credible, or, to use again our seeming paradox, the most natural of events.

The story of the resurrection is *subjectively* the most truthful of narrations. No honest mind can avoid feeling this. These men are telling what they firmly believe to be facts. Such visions were seen, such voices were heard, whether subjective or objective; it would be a wrong to our moral nature to doubt it; such an influence was felt as of one breathing upon them a heavenly power and spirit; whether as undulations of the air without, or proceeding from agitations moving from the spirit within, such words did sound in their ears; they heard them distinctly saying, "Go ye forth and teach all nations, baptizing them in the name of the Father, and of the Son, and of the Holy Ghost." Whether coming, we say, from the inner man, or from outward impressions, these sights, these sounds, these words in their sublime coherence, their heavenly thought, were veritable facts in their psychological experience. They lived in their belief, they conquered in their power, they died in their obedience. Is it held to have been all subjective or imaginative? Be it so. We believe that no honest mind can hold to the inward here and yet long resist the impression of the outward truthfulness. But the first feature is sufficient for the general argument that has been maintained in this book, and, on this account, we are willing to pass by, for the present, those narrations in the gospels that are subsequent to the death of Christ. Aside from its extraordinary yet most natural antecedents, severed from its remarkable consequents, judged simply as a very marvellous event depending merely on such an amount of human testimony, it would present a different aspect, and might, perhaps, rationally allow some degree of honest scepticism. It might be ascribed to a variety of outward and inward impressions without making it thus a greater wonder than would be the admission of its actual objective truth. But such is far from being the case before us. It had these strange antecedents, it had these wondrous, and, except on one supposition, inexplicable consequents. To these, therefore, let us pass, in accordance with the method steadily pursued of making the natural, the human, or the anthropopathic in the Scriptures, the ground-work of the entire and continuous argument.

"He was crucified, dead and buried." And here the remarkable history we have traced so far might seem to have come to a sudden termination, or rather, to present a most mysterious chasm. Comparatively might this be said with truth, although there is a narrow line of continuance contained in the book called "The Acts of the Apostles," and the scanty records it gives us, confined mainly to a portion of the labors of but one, and he the last commissioned of the Christian messengers. Has it occurred to the reader how little is told us anywhere of the other apostles, and how very small a part this book must be of the whole history of the establishment of Christ's kingdom on earth? *A priori* we must believe that the solemn commission did not remain a dead letter, but must have been most faithfully and extensively fulfilled. The remains of ecclesiastical tradition, above all the labors unrecorded yet proved by their effects, the new life everywhere made known, the churches planted from Malabar to Britain, from the Goths to the Arabians and Abyssinians, attest the presence of other messengers, but of the same message, the same preaching, the same story of the cross, the same central doctrine of one who had risen from the dead, and become a newly risen life in all who received him into their souls by faith ; but of all this there are no authentic contemporary records. Leaving out, then, for the present, this narrow stream which we find in the book of the Acts of the Apostles, we have, in the main, and for the greater part of the world and of the Church's history, the wondrous fact to which we would here call attention.

"He was crucified, dead and buried." Here, then, with the exception mentioned, begins one of the strangest chasms in history, —the stumbling chasm to some, and yet, to a right view, methinks, more truly marvellous, and thus more faith-confirming, than any filling up, had it been all as fully given as the narrative of Paul in the Acts. But even this soon leaves us. The continuation after Christ left the earth is like a narrow bridge over a strange depth, and even that terminates before it spans half the dark abyss. How little this is, every intelligent reader feels, and yet it is all we have till we come down nearly to the days of Justin Martyr. But what a mighty work had been accomplished between! Our first feeling is that of subdued complaint. Why could not more have been given us of this deeply interesting period? Why could it not have been filled up, if for no other reason, to baffle the Anti-Christian critics who would build in this historical waste their imaginative theories, and find room therein for the dates of their traditionary and apocryphal gospels? But there it stands, the unbridged chasm over which no critical research can find a way. On one side the death and burial of Christ; on the other this new and wondrous life now working such moral miracles in the Roman world. A greater wonder, we repeat it, than any filling up.

The slender narrative alluded to, though extending so little of the way, and so abruptly terminating, is sufficient to show the unearthly spirit, and the irresistible energy of this new power, whilst the silent blank that remains prepares the thoughtful mind for the contemplation of that real marvel, which, though Gibbon could not see it, is, in fact, the greatest miracle in the chronicles of our earth. Here was wrought the greatest change in the ordinary flow of human acts, and human opinions. The dividing of the Red sea, the turning back of the waters of Jordan, did not equal it. Never was there such an apparent effect in the absence of all assignable earthly causes, natural, moral, social, political, or philosophical! Such a transition period stands alone in history. It is like one of those awful pauses in the physical progress, where, in the mighty visible effect, science traces the existence of a new creating power, and yet that power has worked unseen. It hath veiled its operation, until it stands revealed in the new result, the new order of things it has initiated in nature. The new light shows the hidden power. It is more startling than though all along this transition interval there had been a series of visible miraculous displays, linking the old with the new order of things. We come down to the brink of the last traceable causation, and we know that the supernatural, though we see it not, must somewhere have come between, for here is something which the old nature, the old causation, never could have produced. Such is the effect of this blank, or apparent blank, in the Church's history. To the thoughtful mind folios of miracles, and of minute details of apostolical labors, would not produce a deeper feeling of the wonder-working power of God.

It is, too, well worth bearing in mind, that it is this interval which separates the inspired from the human writings of the Church. May we not say, with all reverence, that in this, too, may be discovered marks of a superhuman wisdom? Had there been an uninterrupted continuance of writings, and ecclesiastical annals, there might have been some ground for the argument which would blend them all in one, and place the patristic on the same or a similar ground of authority with the apostolical. This sharp line coming between, or, rather, this impassable interval, was necessary for that feeling of reverence which puts the one class of books at an unapproachable distance from all others. They are parted in time and position, as well as by the awful superiority of thought that characterizes the immediate messengers of Christ. Hence that veneration for the apostolical writings so remarkable in the earliest subsequent writings of the church. In the days of Clement, "Holy Scripture" is quoted as the inspired word of God, separate from all other books, and with as religious a reverence as even now after an awe-creating lapse of eighteen hundred years. Such is the voice of the true tradition, setting aside the claims that are falsely made for it as of equal, or even collateral, authority with the Scriptures. It is, indeed, the earliest and most universal tradition, superseding all other traditions, that the books of the old and new Testaments, the latest of which are the apostolical epistles, stand apart from all human writings however religious,—that they are, in truth, the books that contain, in the most unrivalled degree and manner, the divine faith, or the mind of God as revealed to man.

"He was crucified, dead and buried." We left the Saviour sleeping in the tomb of Joseph. A brief history follows, and then all is dark. Now look down the intervening waste. We discover the light again in the brief writings and still briefer accounts of the earliest fathers. It is enough to show that the world has changed; a new era has begun. The new force has not yet become very visible in political history, but it is beyond all doubt alive and working mightily. It is manifesting itself in signs of portentous change. The ages have taken a step in progress from which they can never wholly go back. Unknown as yet to statesmen and philosophers, the transforming power is introducing elements of thought and feeling that must soon affect the whole outward face as well as the deep foundation of Roman society. Whence came it? From philosophy? That had virtually died generations before; the schools had become barren; it was centuries since they had borne any children like Pythagoras, Socrates, or Plato; the questions discussed by wrangling Stoics and Epicureans were dead scholasticisms; Sophists yet talked of ἀρετή, and disputed about the *summum bonum*, but no one expected that their lives should correspond to their ethical precepts. The whole story is told by Lucian, scoffer as he was against Christianity as well as the old mythology. Did this mighty change originate in any silent working of any political or social movements? These were all tending to anarchy or despotism. Philanthropy hardly existed even in theory, and morality had almost perished from the earth. But a new morning is certainly breaking on the world. The ancient vision is drawing nigh. The New Jerusalem is coming down from Heaven. The "feet of the Messengers are seen on the tops of the mountains." Arise, O City of our God—"Arise, shine, for thy Light is come, and the glory of the Lord is dawning upon thee. For lo! darkness covers the earth, and thick darkness the nations, but the Lord is rising upon thee, and his glory is seen upon thee. And the Gentiles are coming to thy light, and kings to the brightness of thy rising. Lift up thine eyes and see; they are hastening to thee, thy sons from far, thy daughters are carried at thy side; the multitudes of the sea are turning to thee, the powers of the nations are becoming thine." Whence, we may ask again, this new light? It has shone forth from the darkness of that garden sepulchre. Whence this new life? It has come from the tomb of that crucified One. Here was, indeed, a resurrection undeniable. It brings its own attestation; it has come down the stream of ages; it is now with us,—this unearthly power; the books that record its early deeds, the strange doctrines so different from anything conceived by human thought, and which have ever accompanied it—these are still with us, still, as of old, challenging the intellect of the world to account for them on any known natural process of mere human development. In our reason's awe, if not in our sense-wonder, can we still feel the power of this standing miracle; and, thus prepared, it is not difficult for us to believe in the personal resurrection of that divine man from whose grave there has certainly flowed forth such a life-giving, earth-transforming force. Thus prepared, we feel that this resurrection of which the Apostles say so much, must be something more than a figure, more than a mere rationalistic revival of truth however transcendent. Examine it as we find it in its early transition state,—examine it as it appears when the current of the world's history embraces it never more to be lost. It was not such an influence as came forth from the grave of Socrates. It was not a school, a doctrine merely, a system of philosophy. Nothing of this kind, no mere truth, or truths, addressed to the intellect, had ever before possessed, or would then have possessed, the power of thus stirring and transforming the souls of men. It was a real life, and no figure; it was something more than even *divine truth* regarded in its rational and moral effect; it was a *motion* in the world, as real and vital a motion as ever flowed in the physical creations, or in the old humanity. The bearers of this new energy did not regard themselves as merely messengers of truth however high and heavenly. This was, indeed, an important part of their mission, but not its essence. They carry with them him who was not only "the Way and the Truth," but also "the Life." They bring into the world a new vital power and the divinely accompanying grace of dispensing it. It is the life of a man who died that it might be thus imparted. This risen life, risen in the power of the Spirit, risen in the quickening of the flesh, this new humanity, they proclaim, they offer, they actually bring to men. *How* communicated, through what media, organic, sacramental, ineffable—these are questions we leave to others, if others shall ever be able to settle them. It is the great *fact* itself to which attention is called, the great thought we find everywhere in the writings and preaching of Paul, and which presents itself as the strange feature of Christianity when the gospel stream unites with the moving history of the world. The interest taken since the Reformation in the doctrine of Justification by Faith, and the vast importance of its revival from the mediæval semi-paganism, have made us lose sight too much of this stronger and still more essential feature of the early Church theology. Hence has come such a change of language as makes it less easy to understand the Patristic writings. But in the primitive Church it was a reality affecting every other aspect of the Christian truth. Christ was in the Christian, as he was in the Church his earthly body. It was no figure employed to represent a mere following, or discipleship. His life was in their life. Hence his sufferings were their sufferings, his resurrection not only the pledge but the ground of the new life then working in their souls, and destined, eventually, to quicken their mortal bodies; and so his satisfaction to law was their satisfaction, his obedience their obedience, his righteousness their righteousness imputed to them rightly, because it was really theirs as it was really his. They were *Christophori*, Christ-bearers, *Theophori*. How prevalent was this feeling, how universally the idea entered into the mind of the early Church, may be judged from the fact that heathen satirists derided these fanatics, as they were fond of calling them, for the mad notion that they carried their God with them, in their souls.

The new idea had introduced a new mode of speech. Justin Martyr had been educated in the dialectics of Platonism, but how different the style of language employed by him, after his conversion, from that of any school of philosophy? How different the language of the same Justin Martyr, as a disciple of Plato and a disciple of Christ! He was learning the vernacular of the New Jerusalem, that city of our God below,

> "Where Egypt, Tyre, and Greek, and Jew,
> Began their speech and lives anew."

It was indeed new and glorious *truth* to which he had awaked, but this was far from expressing the peculiarity of his new state. It was not merely another system of philosophy he had found. He is now Christophorus, Christ-bearing. The dead man's life, given for the Church, had become his life; he lived henceforth in the risen vitality of the crucified Redeemer.

Εγὼ ἐν αὐτοῖς—"*I in them,*" says the Saviour, in His intercessory prayer. There is the same idea in that frequent language of the Apostle, *ἐν Χριστῷ*, "*in Christ,*" and the corresponding expression ***Χριστὸς ἐν ὑμῖν***, "*Christ in you.*" Are these figures, we ask again, or do they denote the most vital of realities? The relation of a teacher to those who adopted his system of truth, however high, even though it included, as truth merely, the highest verities of the Christian faith,—such a relation would seem to fall below the significance of language so strange, so new, so evidently called out by the exigency of a new and strange idea. It may come very natural to us now to treat it as a figure, but then, it should be remembered, it was without precedent in the world. It had with it no such associations of thought, either for the cultivated or the common mind. The language had never before been heard. *Ἐν Μωσῇ, in Moses*, would have sounded as strange for such a purpose as *ἐν Πλάτωνι, ἐν Ζήνωνι, in Plato,* or *in Zeno.* Discipleship had never been thus expressed before Christ said, "Lo, I am *with you* always, even to the end of the world."

Such, then, was their warrant for going forth; they carried the Saviour with them,—not his teachings, not his truth merely, not his doctrines alone, though it were the doctrine of the cross, not any mere power given to the truth, if we can understand what that means, but Christ himself. Teacher and taught were alike *ἐν Χριστῷ*, and the evidence that the former was a true Apostle came from the fact that his ministrations were followed by this new life in his converts, whether manifested in the outward miraculous gifts, or the more inward sanctifying grace. "Ye seek a *proof* of Christ speaking in me," τοῦ ἐν ἐμοὶ λαλοῦντος Χριστοῦ, says the Apostle, 2 Corinth. xiii, 3 : "Prove your own selves ; know ye not that Jesus Christ is in you unless ye be ἀδόκιμοι, *unproved*—reprobates ?"

This style of speech is not employed in the Old Testament. It can be traced to the influence of no Jewish schools or sects. Neither among Pharisees, nor Sadducees, nor Essenes, is there to be found anything like it. It is as utterly unknown to any Rabbinical as to any classical usage. What then is its fair meaning? May it not be that in modern times we have fallen below it, have treated it too much as a mere figure, or, if it be a figure, have suffered our rationalizing glosses to warp us away from that most inward and vital significance which alone could have demanded and made universal so strange a metaphor ? We venture to say that this is now the great question of the Church. Until this matter of interpretation is settled, our other polemics are comparatively of little importance. Let it be once thus settled in real, and not merely rhetorical, accordance with primitive usage, and many other theological discords might be resolved that now seem utterly unmanageable.

It was certainly something more than a figure to the writer who so extensively employs it. The Pauline language and the Pauline doctrine seem wholly built upon it. From it, too, grows out all the Apostle's personal experience. He talks like a man who would seem to have, in some measure, lost his old personal identity. There is still the continuity of memory and consciousness; the old Adam is indeed well remembered, but along with all this there is a new humanity, as real and as vital as the first. After his conversion he is no longer Saul of Tarsus, but "a man in Christ." "*I know* a man in Christ," he says—so it should be rendered, and not *I knew*—*οἶδα ἄνθρωπον ἐν Χριστῷ*—"I know a man in Christ who was caught up to the third heaven:" "Of such an one will I glory, but of myself (my old self) I will not glory." How few are the verses we can read continuously in the writings of this fervid Christian without finding something to remind us of this idea? Whatever may be the matter or doctrine treated of how soon does it come round to that loved name so constantly identified with his new personal being, *Christ Jesus*, or in his own soft Syriac vernacular, *Yesu Meshiho*, so oft in its occurrence beyond what is to be found in any other parts of the Bible! Place the Pauline epistles where we may, they might be detected, without other proof, by the very sight of this word striking the eye in every page, and in almost every verse. If we are authorized to judge by the force and frequency and tenderness with which he employs it, Christ was in Paul as really and truly as he ever walked by the sea of Galilee, or talked with his disciples in the flesh; as really and truly as he personally died on the cross, and rose again from the dead.

We study Christ in Paul; may we venture to say it? The writer would speak with caution here, and yet the opinion may be advanced, that we learn more of Christ, of the mind and heart of Christ, as he is manifested in this noble Apostle, than in the records of the evangelists themselves. He comes nearer to us, we see him more distinctly, we converse with him more intimately, he is more tender, more human, as thus seen in the "Christ-bearing" disciple, than in his outward words and acts as recorded in the gospel narrations. By such language we do not underrate those precious portions of the Scripture. Christ is near to us, very near to us, as he appears in his life on earth; he is still nearer to us—may we venture to say it?—as he is risen in the Church. As God the Father comes to us in Christ—so may we not venture reverently to say?—Christ comes nigh to us in his holy people, in the souls of true Christians, and, above all, as he is so brightly manifested in the words and acts of him who labored more than all, and who, whilst rejoicing in the new life, was ever willing to give his earthly life for the Lord Jesus.

CHAPTER XVIII.

The Apostle Paul — Compared with other Apostles — The Transformation of Peter — Paul compared with James and John — Paul the Apostle of Faith — James of Works — John of Love — Injustice of this Comparison — The World regards Paul as the Dogmatist — Same Injustice, to some extent, in the Church — The Pauline Ethics — Paul the most practical of Moralists — Abundance of his Ethical Precepts—The Heavenly Love as exhibited by John — As exhibited by Paul. His Picture of Charity — The exuberant Tenderness of his Language—The Pauline Philanthropy — Compared with the Secular — Incidents in the Apostle's Life and Labors — Their Truthfulness — Paul no Fanatic — His Moderation — His Preference of the Moral to the Miraculous — Thinks more of Charity than of Gifts — The Ideal unexplained by the Corresponding Actual a greater Miracle than the Actual itself. Strauss to be met on his own ground.

The labors and writings of the other Apostles would furnish like examples of this new soul-phenomenon. What thoughtful mind, awake to the wonderful in anthropology, can fail to be struck with the difference between the epistles of Peter so glowing with divinest thought, and the narrow self-ignorance,—we might almost say, stupidity,—of the same man when in the immediate company, and enjoying the personal instructions, of the Great Teacher on earth! Peter before and after the day of Pentecost—what a transformation, what a resurrection had intervened! Equally true are these thoughts of all the others; but we have dwelt upon the writings and works of Paul chiefly because of a strong conviction that not only in the world, but in the Church, there has been more or less of personal injustice in the estimate formed of his natural and his Christian character. Among the irreligious Paul is very generally regarded as representing the harsher features of Christianity. Infidels and rationalists are fond of placing him in contrast with Christ; they speak of him as bigoted, intolerant, dogmatic, denunciatory, delighting in the stern and gloomy doctrinal, in distinction from a practical and loving morality,—all this in the face of the fact, which can be so easily tested, that all the Pauline Epistles contain not so much that is condemnatory and severe as some single discourses of the merciful Saviour. And so in the Church; there has been manifested with some a disposition to compare him unfavorably with the Apostle John. Paul is indeed commended; his zeal, his Christian heroism are described in the most glowing terms; it is admitted that he was "the man for the times." But then he is set forth as the Apostle of faith, of dogmas, and these, too, of the harsher kind, whilst James is the representative of practical morality, and John of the milder and more heavenly principle of love.

But surely there is a great mistake here. Certain habits of thought have led good men, and even profound men, into comparisons that seem wholly unwarranted when we examine, for that purpose, the writings and histories of the blessed servants of Christ. It may be thought irreverent to have any preferences among them; each has his own peculiar Christian excellence; but an impartial examination would show that the practical ethical precepts of Paul not only exceed those of James, but of all the writers of the New Testament, Evangelists and Apostles combined. Sublime as is the Sermon on the Mount, holy as it is in every line and letter, yet is there about it an air of authority; it has a preceptual, ethical form; and these, whilst they render it more majestic, more commanding, more divine, do also—we would say it with all reverence—make it less human, less tender, than those chapters of Romans and Ephesians where the spirit of these heavenly canons so lovingly appears in the most moving exhortations to the daily Christian life. There it was Christ the Lawgiver, the Prophet, the Master, the Great Teacher; here it is Christ the risen Saviour, Christ in Paul, giving the same precepts to a beloved Church, recognized as his own members, his own living body, deriving its ethical life from Him as its own living Head.

Paul, it is said, is the representative of faith—John, of love. Such a contrast is unjust to both. Each of them, it may rather be held, represents that "faith which works by love," and that love which faith in the risen life of the Crucified elevates into a vital affection of fraternity, far transcending any abstract benevolence grounded on secular ideas or any merely secular reasoning. In the beloved apostle, this holy affection takes more of the quietistic form. It is paternal rather than fraternal. It is a sweet and calm emotion, having more of the purely heavenly, and less of that *divine-human* which so powerfully affects us, or should affect us, in the burning words of Paul. Nowhere else in the Scriptures, unless we except the declarations of the Saviour's love, can there be found language of such exquisite tenderness. And it is everywhere. Hardly can there be found a doctrine, a precept, an exhortation, an interpretation, from which the writer does not soon turn to express his love to Christ; and nearly as frequent is the exhibition of the same language towards those whom he believes to be *in Christ*, his spiritual kinsmen, his very dear brethren, yea, nearer than brethren in the natural humanity, even members of the same spiritual body, partakers of the same heavenly life as derived from the same risen and exalted Head. The language of John is general; it specifies not those relations in which the emotion of Christian love has its peculiarly human intensity. Along with its delightful simplicity, it has something of the rapt and mystic air. "Little children, love one another: he that loveth his brother abideth in the light: he that loveth not, abideth in death. We know that we have passed from death to life because we love the brethren: Beloved, let us love one another, for love is of God, and every one that loveth is born of God, and knoweth God: he that loveth not knoweth not God; for God is love." Here is the transcending height of the wrapt contemplative soul. But Paul describes the same divine affection by its human motions in the Christian consciousness. How heavenly and yet how near to our human hearts is such language as this: "Love suffereth long and is kind; love envieth not, vaunteth not itself, is not puffed up; love seeketh not her own, thinketh no evil; beareth all things, believeth all things, hopeth all things, endureth all things; love never faileth." Or he sets forth these throbbings of the new life as the opposites of the old human selfishness and malevolence: "Let all bitterness, and wrath, and anger, and clamor, and evil-speaking, be put away from you with all malice: and be ye kind one to another, tender-hearted, forgiving one another, even as God, for Christ's sake, hath forgiven you." Again, they are presented to us as the richest growth of the heavenly grace: For the fruit of the spirit is love," and with love come "joy, peace, long-suffering, gentleness, goodness, faith; that *Christ may dwell in your hearts* by faith; that ye, being rooted in love, and built on the foundation of love, may be able to comprehend, with all saints, what is the length, and breadth, and depth, and height of love, and to know that love of Christ which passeth knowledge; that ye might be filled with all the fulness of God." This the language of the dogmatist, of the harsh preacher of an antinomian faith! How unjustly, how ignorantly, do the world, and many professedly in the Church, judge of this noble servant of Jesus! He has been regarded as the austere apostle, but how he loved even his persecuting brethren the Jews! Hear him, too, how he pours out his soul in love for Christians, and especially his spiritual children in Christ: "For we were gentle in the midst of you, even as a nurse nourisheth her children; thus longing for you, *ἱμειρόμενοι*, being affectionately desirous of you, we were willing to impart unto you not only the gospel of God, but our own souls, because ye were *ἀγαπητοί*, very dear unto us; and ye are witnesses, and God is witness, how holily, and righteously, and unblamably we behaved ourselves among you that believed."

But in all this there is another question than the personal character of Paul. It has reference to the origin of these divine ideas, and these new emotions associated with them,—this new love to man so born of the still deeper love to a crucified and risen Redeemer: "Christ in you the hope of glory:" "For your life is hid with Christ in God, and when Christ who is your life, shall appear, then shall ye also appear with him in glory:" ζῶ δὲ οὐκ ἔτι ἐγὼ, ζῇ δὲ ἐν ἐμοὶ Χριστὸς;* "I live, yet no longer I, it is Christ that liveth in me." Where did Paul get this divine thought, so far transcending Plato, of a new and heavenly life lived here on earth, ἐν τῇ θνητῇ σαρκὶ, "in this our mortal flesh?"† In what school of philosophy did he learn this psychological mys-

* Galat. ii., 20. † 2 Corinth. iv., 11.

tery of a new humanity, connecting itself vitally with the old manhood, and elevating it to its own celestial sphere, so that Christians here might have their "citizenship" with the Ecclesia above, and thus "be made to sit together in heavenly places in Christ Jesus?" Call them figures if you will, still the wonder remains; whence these unearthly figures, and these unearthly doctrines demanding a language so unknown to all the world before? There is but one answer to these questions, and on that answer is grounded the immovable evidence of Christianity and the Scriptures.

It is worthy of remark, how, in the hands of Paul, even the secular, or merely ethical, benevolence rises to a higher spiritual degree. As modified by the new life, and the new idea, it is no longer the *barren* earthly philanthropy. Utilitarian it may still be called, but it is the transcendental or heavenly utilities it now brings with it, and which so distinguish it from any classical or heathen virtue, as well as from any modern casuistry that may claim the name. It is the celestial Ἔρως, the immortal Love, the love-producing love, the virtue-bearing virtue, the Grace the mother of other graces. The dead antinomian faith says, "Be ye warmed, be ye clothed, but giveth not; the secular philanthropy gives warmth to the body, clothing to the earthly nakedness;—it strives to make men comfortable, and in confining itself to this, may ofttimes breed that very worldliness in which itself as well as all higher charity expires. But the Pauline benevolence, the Christian benevolence, warms the soul. The secular becomes the subordinate value, and, in this way, paradoxical as it may seem, is actually increased by being made subordinate, whilst the heavenly utility appears in the new virtue, the new grace it generates, or tends to generate, in both the giver and the recipient. How sublimely does the Scripture charity here rise above that of any classical or heathen morals! Surely must a soul be blind not to see that there had now come into the world a new light, a new love, a new and heavenly principle of action. Its great value is not so much its worldly good as its spiritual reproductiveness. It produces love in other souls, and, thus regarded as a state of the spirit, is a higher thing and of higher worth than happiness, though necessarily connected with it. Charity enriches the giver with grace, and makes the recipient a better man. It cherishes devotion, it strengthens faith, brings out a rich harvest of thanksgiving to God, and thus contributes to that great end of moral action, —the divine glory. Beautifully is all this set forth by Paul (2 Corinthians ix, 12); it is in fact the idea which renders clear a passage that has seemed to some commentators to present no little obscurity: "For the administration of this service (this almsgiving) not only supplieth the wants of the saints, but superabounds (περισσεύουσα) through many thanksgivings to God; whilst, by their experience of this ministration, they *glorify* God for your subjection to the Gospel of Christ, and for your liberal distribution unto them and to all men; and by their *prayer* for you as they *long after you* (ἐπιποθούντων ὑμᾶς), loving you dearly, on account of the exceeding grace of God in you: thanks be unto God for his unspeakable gift." How different the motives for this almsgiving, how different, too, the benefits enumerated, from those of the ordinary, secular or utilitarian benevolence! The thought of happiness, or of any worldly comfort, almost wholly disappears. It is lost in the glory of the higher ideas that come welling up from this "*super*-abounding" fountain,—the thanksgiving, the glorifying, the prayer, the tender love. We see, too, the train of thought that led Paul at the close to break out in the rapturous exclamation—"Thanks be unto God for his unspeakable gift,"—the gift of Christ, God's merciful alms to a poor perishing world. From this gift of Christ comes the life that warms them all, the generative power that makes this one virtue of almsgiving the mother of so many others. The gift of Christ,—it rescues us from perdition, it saves us from pain, it is a source of the purest happiness ; but more than all—and this was the ineffable value that rose highest in the Apostle's mind—it creates the richest virtue in the human soul, and thus abounds, and "superabounds, to the glory of God."

No part of the Scriptures would furnish better examples of that outward naturalness and truthfulness on which we have so much insisted than the "Acts of the Apostles," and especially those parts that give us, with so much lifelikeness of coloring and detail, the labors of Paul. If space allowed to dwell upon them, we might refer to almost every point in his career. How real is every picture! Paul at the feet of Gamaliel, Paul the zealous Pharisee, Paul at the stoning of Stephen, Paul on his way to Damascus,

Paul seeing visions and a light from heaven; whether subjectively or objectively, we inquire not now, but when was a vision ever more truthfully narrated? Or turn we to his new life: Paul kneeling before Ananias, Paul praying, receiving baptism, speaking "straightway with boldness in the name of the Lord Jesus,"—Paul with the brethren at Jerusalem, again seeing Christ in the temple vision, journeying on his new mission to Antioch, sent forth to the cities of Asia Minor, reading in the Synagogue on the Sabbath day, now worshipped as a messenger from heaven, then stoned and left for dead by the wayside,—Paul withstanding Peter to his face, contending with Barnabas, distrusting Mark, departing with Silas,—"Paul in perils by land, in perils by water, in stripes, in imprisonments, in tumults, in fastings, troubled on every side, yet not distressed, always bearing about in the body the dying of the Lord Jesus,"—Paul by the sea-shore at Troas, musing on the shaping destiny that seemed, in spite of all his purposes, to direct his mighty mission to the opposite-lying coast of Europe,—Paul seeing by night the man of Macedonia standing by him and saying, "cross over and help us,"—Paul at Athens disputing with the philosophers, at Ephesus in the midst of the raging mob, at Miletus kneeling on the beach and praying with the elders of the Church,—Paul at Jerusalem rescued by the Roman captain, speaking to the people in his own Hebrew tongue, pleading his cause before Felix,—in all these circumstances displaying that manly truthfulness which ever won for him the favor of the stern Roman authorities,—Paul in the deep, a prisoner in chains, yet rising through the greatness of his spiritual strength to the actual command of the foundering vessel;—plain outward facts all of them; how objectively graphic in their narration, and yet how suggestive, how full of soul! An uninspired writer, especially a modern one, would have inverted the pictures, turned them inside out, as it were. He would, perhaps, have filled his pages with Paul's "subjective," as it is called. He would have given his religious experience. He would have told us all how he *felt*, and what he *thought*, as he stood on Mars Hill, or what great conceptions filled his soul as he drew near the mighty city of the Seven Mountains. And yet what lets us more readily and clearly into the inward character and state of the man, than the simple objective style of the Scripture narrative? We have before our eyes, and distinctly conceived in our thought, this most remarkable person in every stage and phase of his old and renewed being: Paul the youthful Pharisee, "haling men to prison," and stoning them to death, yet verily thinking that he was doing God service,—"Paul the aged," looking to his departure, confessing himself the chief of sinners, yet maintaining the earnestness and sincerity with which he had run the Christian race, and fought the fight of faith,—Paul, of whom even after his conversion, it might be thought that no one would be more likely to prove a fanatic, or a rash enthusiast, yet, instead of this, ever the man of loving moderation, who was willing, in the noblest sense, to be all things to all men if so be that he could win souls to Christ,—Paul the ardent, the excitable, the vision-seeing, and who, it might be thought, would have delighted in the miraculous, the wonder-making, yet, on the contrary, ever preferring the moral and spiritual, however sober, to the marvellous, however tempting to the religious imagination :—so truthful was he, so loving, so just in the midst of excitements that might have affected the strongest unsupported reason. He could speak with tongues more than they all ; he magnified the miraculous gifts with which God had endowed the Church, even where he turns from them and says, "yet show I unto you a more excellent way." Then follows that picture of Charity before alluded to, that heavenly limning, by which alone, if men had eyes to see, and hearts to feel, might be tested the inspiration of the human soul that conceived it, and the divinity of the Scriptures in which it is contained.

We do not underrate physical miracles, when we say they are less wonderful than such a character. What influence on earth, what school on earth, Oriental, Occidental, Greek, Roman, Jewish, could have "developed" the Apostle Paul as he appears in this his own strange transition age? We might rest the evidence of Christianity, as it has been most ably and convincingly rested, on the utter impossibility of explaining this mystery in the human in any other way than by the supernatural and divine.

The Straussian men should be met on their own ground. Given the ideal to account for it,—this is the problem. We have the ideal Christ, the ideal Paul, the ideal Christian Church with its superhuman doctrines. They are before us in history, they are now with us in books, they are seen and felt in the world. There is no known earthly development to which they can be assigned. Why then should we hesitate to admit the divine and the unearthly as manifested in some corresponding actual? The former without the latter is only the greater wonder. It has the doubly miraculous, its own exceeding strangeness, and the utter inexplicability of its human origin.

CHAPTER XIX.

APPLICATION OF THE ARGUMENT — THE BIBLE A WORLD-BOOK— Summation of the Argument from the Natural — Such an Exhibition of the Human could not have been without the Superhuman — The Jewish as compared with the Greek and Roman History — The Bible Catholicism in its Adaptation to individual States of individual Souls — Moses nearer to us, notwithstanding his Orientalism, than the Greek and Roman Legislators — The Bible Hebrew as compared with the Greek and Latin — The Remarkable Intelligibility of the Bible Hebrew in the Letter — Surpassing, in this respect, the other Shemitic tongues, though aided in its Interpretation by them — Two Reasons of this—The Breath of the Lord inspiring it — A Second Reason, the intense Humanity of its Images.

THE Scriptures furnish an inexhaustible mine of illustration for the purposes of our argument; but the rapid sketches that have been given are sufficient to satisfy any thoughtful mind, that in the book itself, in its "peculiar people" so remarkably connected with the whole destiny of the race, in its history so strange yet so truthful, in its doctrines so unearthly yet given through language so intensely human, in its wonderful position in the very heart of human culture, in its sudden power when newly brought to bear upon the mind and conscience of an age, and in the lasting tenacity of its influence upon the world's best and highest thinking, there is, indeed, a mystery which can be solved by no explanation short of the supernatural and the divine. Thus, then, we say in conclusion, take the whole Bible, leave out its supernatural—that is, its supernatural in outward act—fix the mind upon its earthly history, its unique consistency, its ancient βουλὴ or Oracular Messianic purpose so early proclaimed and so steadily maintained throughout, — let the thought dwell upon its inherent truthfulness, its strong human probabilities, in a word, its great naturalness, and we have before us that position which for philosophic wonder, if we may use the term, the wonder of the thought or reason, surpasses any *sense*-confounding marvel of the outward supernatural itself.

For the supernatural is credible; there are times conceivable when the absence of it would be more strange than its presence; but such a history, though so natural and credible in its *parts,* is yet, without the supernatural as its explanation, incredible as a *whole,* or would be incredible if there were not the strongest evidence of its outward actuality; and this we undeniably have, for here are the books, and the people of whom we speak, and the Church that has been built upon them, and the present history, and the many centuries of past history that have been shaped and made what they are mainly by the power that is in these books, or by other powers which find their explanation nowhere else than in these revelations of humanity to itself.

Such a people as the Israelites, so strange in their secluded history, yet so purely human and natural in their national life, so cut off from the world's general polity, yet with a destiny, so connected with the highest historical development of the race, a destiny announced in the earliest prophecy, and which the whole course of time has been fulfilling,(11)—such a separate people, in this sense, and to this end called "holy,"* did exist; all history has been affected by them; they exist now as a distinct people, though such a fact, strange as it may be, is really the inferior wonder; they yet exist, still more vividly and emphatically, in the mighty power of the past; we have their books, their literature, their poetry, their ethics, their theology, their most stirring national life; it lies in the bosom of all that is best known of the world's culture; it would almost seem from the very course of events, ancient and modern, and even aside from the "sure word of prophecy," as though the whole human race had been created for the very purpose of bringing out the great truths of which this people were made the early, and for a

* Exodus xxii, 31, "And ye shall be holy men unto me." Viri sancti eritis mihi.

long time the only, witnesses. Now we may say that, excepting the outward supernatural, if we choose to except it, the general worldly certainty attending the annals of this strange nation is equal to any that belongs to Greek or Roman history; in intrinsic truthfulness, it may be maintained, it far exceeds them. This, then, being admitted, as beyond any reasonable doubt of any reasonable mind, what is there rationally incredible in the thought that such a people ever carrying with them such a world-destiny, should be the objects of an extraordinary divine care,—if there is any divine care, or if such an idea is credible at all in reference to any earthly object? Why so opposed to any strangeness in nature, if we are compelled to admit the higher strangeness in the historical? In other words, if we can come thus far, if there has been such historical superintendence, general or special, then again, what is there incredible in the statement that the curtain of the natural has been sometimes drawn aside, and God revealed "holding the winds, that they blow not," or "sending them forth as his messengers," or coming "in the flaming fire," or speaking in the "still small voice," when some event, known to him as connected with the world's destiny, demanded the one or the other manifestation?

In the views that have been presented, we see at least the reason of the wondrous catholicism of the Scriptures. We see how it is that they so adapt themselves to the common knowledge, and common thinking, and common imagination, of all men. This is felt the more the book is studied and understood. The effect indeed may be heightened by the elucidating labors of the scholiast and the archæologist; all such clearing of the letter does, for the spiritual mind, add to the spiritual power; but without such helps, or with the scantiest supply of them, and in the poorest translation ever made, it has a fountain of living thought never failing in its rich suggestiveness for the devout unlearned, and never exhausted by any amount of research on the part of the profoundest scholar.

There is another aspect still of this remarkable universality. Not only is the Bible adapted to all ages, to all peoples, to all individuals; it also addresses itself to the most special circumstances of each single soul. Men may doubt this who have never made the Scriptures their study, who, perhaps, seldom read them at all; but still there is no fact better attested in all the range of Baconian or inductive science. The most learned as well as the most simple, have borne witness to it. It is a truth established that there *is* this peculiar life in the world, a life manifesting itself in immense variety of effect, yet equally powerful for mental conditions the most extreme in rank and knowledge. It is all true, the picture that Burns has drawn of the holy influence of the Bible by the cotter's humble hearth; it is all true, what we often hear, and our eyes have witnessed, of its transforming power over the illiterate, of the elevation of thought and feeling it gives to intellects otherwise obtuse, and, not unfrequently, to the rudest savage soul. No other book does this ; but the Bible, wherever it goes, is ever followed by some examples of this strange effect ; let the inductive philosopher put it in his crucible, or his crucial analysis, and explain the phenomenon as he best can. Surely it is as interesting, and demands as much attention, as some of the wonders of chemistry or geology. But much more than this is true. Men profoundly learned in the Scriptures, and in all that wide field of knowledge that relates to them, have not been prevented by their critical and philological investigations from feeling the same quickening spiritual energy of the Word. Bible scholars like Usher, classical scholars like Erasmus, philosophers like Bacon, divines like Edwards, metaphysicians like Leibnitz and Hamilton, men of loftiest scientific as well as spiritual insight like Pascal, men of highest human culture like Wilberforce and Guizot, have sought knowledge, not merely historical, or literary, or speculative, but soul-saving knowledge, from this fountain so full and running over for all. As the child sits down to learn his lesson from the lips of a beloved teacher, so have they betaken themselves to the study of the Scriptures, with the deep conviction that in their human was to be found the superhuman and the divine. They have not merely prized them as ancient writings of rare antiquarian interest, or as connected with some of the most interesting questions of history and ethnology, or as suggestive, oftentimes, of what is deepest in philosophy, richest in poetry, most rare and beautiful in literary criticism; all of these and more than these have they found in this treasure of things new and old, but none of them, nor all of them conbined, have formed its chief attraction. With reverence have they bowed their heads upon the sacred volume, acknowledging it to be Holy Scripture in no conventional sense, but as having truly come to us in our humanity from a superhuman holy source. With all lowly submission, as to a divine voice speaking through human organs, have they listened for what God would say unto their individual souls, as adapted to their own individual experience. No want of knowledge in the infidel, no self-ignorance in the pretentious rationalist, can make false the fair induction to be drawn from this so varied inward testimony. Their superficial acquaintance with the Scriptures cannot nullify this experience of the most cultivated as well as the most unnurtured minds, or make void the fact, so far surpassing in wonder any mere physical phenomenon, that there has been for many ages, and still is, in our world, this mighty and most catholic spiritual power.

The peculiarity of the Scriptures on which we have been dwelling is certainly a remarkable one, let the sceptic explain it as he may. Whether taken in its religious or its literary aspect, it is certainly true that in this character of universality no other book can be compared with the Bible. Homer, perhaps, comes nearest to it in this feature, but at what an immense distance! Will any one refer to the Greek and Roman ounders for whom, too, there has been claimed a sort of inspiration? Let us look at it. Historically, ethnologically, politically, they are nearer to us, much nearer to us, than the Oriental Lawgiver; but spiritually, humanly, in all that concerns our truest, our most central manhood, how much more akin to us is Moses than Lycurgus or Numa? How much better we understand—not his writings merely, but his humanity as one with our humanity. How much more does he enter, not only into the religion, but into the literature, the legislation, in a word, the whole thinking of our modern society, than any influence that has descended from Greek or Roman books. This, it might be said, has come from a peculiar course of events;

but that would be making history a matter of chance. It is not a mere misplacing accident that has caused it; this course of events has been itself one effect of this peculiar power; and yet, had the question been asked, two centuries before the Christian era, what literature, two thousand years hence, would have the most influence in the world, what mind among the many acute minds of that period would have turned to the secluded hills of Judea? In like manner are their languages, etymologically, syntactically, more nearly related to our own; and yet, in regard to this interior or more catholic manhood, how foreign, how barbarous, may we say, their copious Greek and Latin, as compared with the power of his own scanty yet clear and lofty Hebrew! How much more obscure, too, oftentimes, as well as feeble are they, notwithstanding their greater culture, and their more abundant means of rhetorical expression.

There is a thought here well worth our

attention, in its bearing on what we have called the Divine human in the Scriptures. It is the remarkable intelligibility of the Bible Hebrew. The reference, in this apparent paradox, is not to the ineffable doctrine. Here, indeed, is difficulty; here is a demand for study surpassing that required for any science, any philosophy, of earth. We mean the intelligibility of the letter all the way down to where it is lost in the spiritual, the pure humanness of the media through which the Divine ideas are approximated to us, the verbal lucidity, clearness of style, cleanness of figure, transparency, we might call it, of radical and etymological imagery. With the exception of a very few Phœnician fragments, the Old Testament is the only writing extant in the ancient Hebrew; and yet, even without the cognate tongues that have only of late been extensively called in aid, how very little is there that could be truly pronounced unintelligible, in that sense of intelligibility that has been mentioned! But let us imagine, on the other hand, that Homer, even the graphic, picture-making Homer, had been our only surviving relic of the Greek,—or the exact, word-weighing Lucretius our only remains of the Latin, what immense lacunæ, or series of equally worthless conjectures, must have existed in the best translations; how much would be beyond the recovering power of all the scholiasts, and that, too, not merely in matters of local and partial allusion, but in the expression of the most ordinary and general thought.

It is not, however, merely in the Hebrew as a language that we find the grounds of this comparison. There is, in truth, in this ancient tongue, a sharp outline significance, a remarkable defining power, as we may call it; yet, still *mere* human compositions, had they been written in it and been preserved to us, would doubtless have presented, in many respects, the same feebleness and common-place obscurities—obscure because they are common-place—that meet us in other literature. The daughter dialect of the Rabbinical, though vastly more copious, has become trifling, and, of consequence, unmeaning, in the Talmud; shelves are filled with the obscure drivel that has been written in the near cognate Syriac; even the nobler Arabic has lost greatly in respect to its ancient clearness, and abounds in ambiguities and obscure conceits, whose mastery will not pay one often for the pains taken in their elucidation. Everywhere else has this grand Shemitic stock degenerated. Not in the language, therefore, as such (we mean in the language radically as distinguished from other tongues near or remote) must we seek the sole explanation of this original power, as we find it in the Bible. There is one thought alone that solves the mystery, that gives the full reason of that remarkable intelligibility which has been noticed by the profoundest scholars. It is the Divine breath in these old

Scriptures that has filled them so full of life; it is the Divine voice of authority, sounding in every page, that has given them this wonderful and otherwise inexplicable clearness. It is because it is "the Word of God, sharper than any two-edged sword, reaching even to the dividing of soul and sense, the joints and the marrow, a critic both of the *thinkings* and the *ideas* of the heart." "It is the lamp of the Lord, which like the breath of man" (in the physical organization), "searches all the inward chambers of" the soul.*

Add to this what has been so much insisted on, the intense humanity of the Old Scriptures, and we have another reason why this very ancient and most peculiarly Oriental tongue so vividly pours out its thought, and is so translatable, into the most remotely varying languages of the modern Western world.

* Prov. xx, 27.

CHAPTER XX.

The Power of the Bible — The Effect of the Scriptures not merely from our Familiarity with them — The Power of the Written Word as shown at the Reformation — Similar to the effect on the Roman World, and in the Patristic Period — The "Finding of the Book of the Law" as when found by Hilkiah the Priest — So the Bible went forth from the Cell of the Augustine Monk — The Power is in the Book itself — The Hebrew Prophets — How they talk to our Age — The Imprecatory Psalms — Still needed in the Church's Liturgy — The Book of the Race — The Old Family Bible — Contains our Natural and Spiritual Genealogy — Contains the Ideas of the race that are most Universal — Such as the Fall, Redemption, Incarnation, the Human Brotherhood — Men who compare the Scriptures with other Books called "Sacred" — Difficulties in the Bible — The Fight of Faith — Two Kinds of Scepticism — Accommodations — The Question again asked: Are the Modern Rationalists making Progress in Holiness? — Worthlessness of their Criticism.

It might be said that this effect of the Hebrew writings was owing to the long familiarity of reverent religious associations. But such an account of the matter will not stand the test either of reason or of facts. It is putting the effect for the cause. It fails to explain the first power and the long tenacity. The Scriptures have had the same influence, and manifested it much more strikingly, when first presented to an age or people,—and that, too, not its first recipients, but a new age or people far removed and far different, both in history and culture. We have already alluded to their power in the Patristic period, when they burst upon the new-born mind of the Church, and newly encountered the utterly alien feeling of the Roman world. Thus was it also in the Reformation age, after the whole Bible had for a second time been so long buried from the common mind. As when Hilkiah the priest discovered in the temple a copy of the law that the Lord had given unto Moses, so came forth the Scriptures from the cell of the Augustine monk. Men everywhere, great men and mean men, learned men and ignorant men, "wept and humbled themselves at the reading of the words of the book that was found." What a sudden activity did it give, not only to the religious, but to all the higher departments of thinking. How it quickened the age! How it made the theological and the spiritual predominant everywhere, in the political, social, and even military life! How paradoxically, we may say, yet how truly, did this strangely human book, with its abounding anthropopathisms, engage the general mind in the highest heights of abstract speculation,—as though this very anthropopathism, more than any philosophical language, contained those hidden germs that must grow up evermore into the infinity of thought.

The power, we say, is in the book itself, and not merely in its historical associations, or the reverence of early belief, or its long familiar sacredness. To feel it fully, it is even necessary, sometimes, to get rid of this familiarity, by reading the Scriptures from some new standpoint. We must study the books of Moses in connection with the nearest contemporary writings, thus transplanting ourselves into the old life of each ; and then it will be seen that there is in the Jewish Legislator a world-life that cannot, by any alchemy of association, or revivification, be again recovered from any institutes of like antiquity.

We need not dwell on this universality as found in the Psalms of David. Devout feeling and the most learned critical research alike concur in the thought that the key to their best interpretation is found in that view which regards them as the divine songs of all truly religious souls, the standing temple service of all ages, so adapted to the expression of temporal and spiritual sorrows, temporal and spiritual joys, temporal and spiritual triumphs, temporal and spiritual salvation, that each may be regarded as the primary or secondary significance, according to the state of soul in which the recipient reads or chants the wondrously adapted words. There is nowhere in the physical world any such evidence of adaptedness or design as this. The historical world certainly furnishes nothing like it. Let it be called accommodation, if any prefer the word ; we could not thus accommodate one of the lyric hymns of Greece, or a song of the Rig Veda. In these, it is true, there are strains of conflict, of deliverance, of triumph,—there is, moreover, the representation of the superhuman and the supernatural,—but then there is wholly lacking that idea which overlooks all differences of outward human condition, or of human wants, in the nearness of the divine personal presence,—the idea of help from the one God, all mighty, all holy, dwelling in the highest heavens, yet ever nigh the soul that calleth on him.

It is this idea, made alive by faith, that characterizes the Bible prayer, and the Bible salvation, whether it be of the temporal or spiritual kind. To the Greek, religion was a matter of taste, of beauty, of artistic fancy ; to the Hindoo, it was a mystic contemplation for the higher, a grotesque monstrosity, or a horrid diversion, for the vulgar mind. To the Christian, as to the Jew, it is a *want* of the soul, a want of God, an urgent need of divine help. There may be, in its Jewish exhibition, more reference to the temporal, as we style it, or the immediate life, as in the Christian, a higher looking to the spiritual deliverance, yet in each is it the same God, the same faith, and thus, as far as its author and object are concerned, essentially the same salvation. Abraham trusted God in temporal promises, and "it was counted to him for righteousness;" for it was a whole trust, a trust for all he knew of his relations to the Invisible, for all he hoped in respect to his total being, whether this present earthly life with a blank beyond, or some unknown as yet unrevealed existence where the weary, rest-seeking pilgrim though dead might yet, in some way, "live unto God." It was a *whole* trust, and, therefore, though having its conceptual limit on earth, it was really a trust for eternity. "These all died in faith, not having received the promises, but seeing them afar, and confessing that they were strangers and travellers upon the earth." Religion was not their æsthetic fancy, their philosophy, their mythic wonder, or even their mystic quietism, but their souls' urgent want; they desired God, as a present help in time of trouble; "they endured as seeing Him who is invisible."

The same idea of the Scripture adaptedness is suggested by the Hebrew prophets. How plain they talk to us, how easily we understand their essential message, when taken out of its partial aspects of time and place! We know well the chronological periods of their predictions; we are not at all ignorant of their primary applications, nor of the peculiar, the very peculiar, historical states that furnish the ground of their impassioned admonitions; most special indeed, most exclusive are they in their national and ethical aspects; and yet we cannot help feeling that these ancient Seers are talking to *us*, talking to all men, to all ages. Their words are just the words, just the figures, which are needed now, and found to be most appropriate now, in rebuking every form of wrong, of oppression, of public or private wickedness. If any part of the Bible belongs to a past age, it would seem to be the imprecatory prayers of the Psalms. At least, it might be said a later revelation has abrogated their use. And yet there are times now, and men now, and transactions now taking place upon the earth, and wrongs and enormities still heard of, in reference to which these prayers would seem to be still wanted as the most appropriate language. All other speech fails to express the righteous indignation so different from the personal revenge. It demands its own appropriate language, and the ethical want finds its true relief in these portions of the Church's immutable liturgy: "Oh! crush the oppressor, Lord; arise, my God, lift up thine hand, forget not the humble:" "Break thou the arm of the wicked and evil man; for thou hast smitten our enemies upon the cheek, thou hast broken the teeth of the ungodly:" "Let them fall by their own counsels, cast them out in the multitude of their transgressions, for they have rebelled against thee:" "But let those that put their trust in thee rejoice; let them say, continually, The Lord be magnified, even all such as love thy salvation."

Is it necessary to fortify our positions by referring to the discourses of Christ? When shall this voice become obsolete, or cease to be recognized as the voice of a world-messenger? "No man ever spake like this man,"—ever spake thus to all men, or is so understood by all men. Who thinks of orientalisms, or is critically troubled about orientalisms, when deeply intent on words so human and yet so superhuman, so adapted to the East, yet so intelligible in the West, so marked by the style of the age in which they are uttered, and yet so in unison with the speech and thinking of all ages! Well may the Scriptures be called "THE BOOK." It is the Book of the race. It is the *old* family Bible, long entrusted to the keeping of the *first born*, but where all may come and find their natal record. Here is the historical genealogy of all nations. Compare, in this respect, the simple, truthful, modest ethnology of Genesis with other oriental writings, and with those monstrous legends of theirs that are so out of all proportion with themselves, and all other history. Here, too, is the spiritual genealogy of human souls,—the generation and the regeneration, the man of the earth and the "man from heaven," the *humanity*, or the life in Adam, the *Christianity*, or the life in Christ. Here is "the image of the earthly," and here is "the image of the Heavenly." Here, moreover, is that which belongs to all men as men, the ideas that above all others are the property of the race. Here is the fall, the redemption, the brotherhood in ruin as the ground of all true human sympathy, the brotherhood in grace as the ground of all true human hope, the acknowledgment of the supernatural in both as the true foundation of all genuine philanthropy.

And yet there are men,—men, too, claiming to be intelligent and philosophical,—who will deliberately put these wondrous writings on a par with Chinese and Hindoo oracles. They have never studied them, to be sure, —they know as little of the Scriptures as they do of the Vedas and Shasters of which they talk so flippantly,—and yet they not only name them together as belonging to one general class of "Sacred Books," but seem even to take a strange delight in giving the Bible a secondary place as compared with these "venerable authorities." They do this, too, in the face of the clearest proof, if they will but study it, that what is most "venerable" and most remarkable in these compositions is but the obscured image of one ancient revelation, a deeply-fouled copy from that one antique original now in our possession.

What must we think of the heads or hearts of men, who can deal thus with things most sacred? What respect can be entertained either for their morality or their intelligence? There are doubtless great and real difficulties in the Scriptures, as, to a thinking man, there must be great and real difficulties everywhere else, both in the world without and in the world within. Ever more, as such a one thinks on, existence seems more and more strange, until he finds that he must think himself into total darkness, unless there be, in some form, an objective truth, an objective oracle, in the world. The thought, the God-given thought, we believe, that there must be such an oracle, where the Infinite communes with the finite in the finite language,—this holds him up. This leads him to the Scriptures, and yet, even when he feels, in the deepest convictions of his experience, that there is truly a divine voice speaking to him therein, still are there difficulties, great and real difficulties. He must "fight the fight of faith." These ancient books are strange, even as nature is strange, and the world within him, even his own soul, is strange, exceedingly strange; and this he discovers the more and more he knows of its psychological, and especially its moral depths. These ancient books are very different from what he would *at first* have fancied a revelation ought to be; and so, if he keeps on thinking, will he find out mysteries, not merely curious scientific facts or laws, but awful, fathomless mysteries in nature, such as he never would have thought could be contained in her, or have been revealed by her. There is this difference, however, that the farther he goes in the physical, rejecting every other aid, the more he gets involved in darkness as to the meaning of it all; whereas, to the Bible student, there does at last arise a light "with healing in its wings," which he feels to be true light by its self-evidencing power, and by its shedding light on other things. By the aid of this he sees, more and more, that in the construction and plan of this book, there is indeed a superhuman wisdom, —that in its most human utterances there is "a thought which is above our thoughts, and a way that is above our ways." Still are there difficulties in the Scriptures. For the trial of our faith, or because in no other way could the heavenly light be reflected upon our souls, God has suffered shadows to rest upon the mirror. To some spiritual states these may be so magnified in their shapes, and so intensified in their shading, as to render faith a difficult exercise of soul, or only to be sustained by a constant gazing upon those brilliant heights of truth that everywhere stand out of the surrounding mist. The unbelief that arises in such circumstances is not infidelity. It is an unhappy condition of the spirit demanding, instead of intolerance, our earnest prayers, and our deepest sympathy. There are such sceptics entitled to our respect and our love. They do not choose unbelief *per se;* they have enough of the light to make them love it, and long for more of it, notwithstanding the disquiet that is suffered to visit their souls.

But no such plea can be made for those who are evidently fond of these odious parallels, not more profane religiously than they are revolting to all pure and elevated thought. It is hard to be friends with men who can, without compunction, put Jesus and Confucius together, to say nothing of Jesus and Shakspeare; it is hard to feel respect for minds that can see no difference between the Christian Scriptures and the Hindoo books; it is not easy to entertain a sentiment of tolerance for hearts that will place the representations of ineffable holiness, and righteous moral government, and fearful, yet loving personality, such as we find everywhere in the one, on the same level with the pantheistic common-places, the vulgar *gnosis*, the foul nature-worship, and impure symbolism of the other. Is this done knowingly? What must be thought of their appreciation of the pure and the sublime? Is it done as is most probable, in utter personal ignorance of these books, and of the grossness of their spiritually disguised sensualism? What must be thought of the anti-christian hatred that could alone have prompted a parallel as false as it is revolting, as absurd as it is unholy!

There is, however, another attitude, we make bold to say it, that is more irrational, if not more irreverent, than that of either scoffing or scowling unbelief. It is that of the men who profess to regard the Scriptures as in some sense inspired, in some sense a revelation, and yet with an express or tacit reserve that most of these "sacred writings," *Sacræ Scripturæ*, as they conventionally style them, are already obsolete, and the remainder fast becoming obsolete in the advancing light of the world. There are others who profess a more cordial reception, perhaps, yet would they maintain that this respect is due to the thoughts, the "great truths" as they deferentially say, whilst the style, the words, the images, are "accommodations" merely, and, therefore, to be dispensed with by that higher thinking, that can think of God as well, if not better, without them. Accommodations truly! Grant the unmeaning and evasive word; but still accommodations for *us* as well as for past ages; accommodations for us as well as for the Platonists, the Aristotelians, and the Academics of the first century. Accommodations for *us!* And why not then shall we be accommodated by them? Why assume the irreverent attitude of ignoring their benefit as though we had obtained some lofty position, or—as it has been shown before, that this claim of progress must mean, if it mean anything to the purpose — some superlatively holy height, some earth-removing, heaven-nearing height, that enables us to look down upon these humble stepping-stones for the feet of the lower and more worldly-minded traveller.

They were well enough in their day; they are well enough for others; but *we* see *through* them; we have become so spiritually-minded, so unworldly, that we see without them; they are hindrances now rather than helps to the advanced philosophic intuition; the great problems of life and destiny are all solved; we have the modern literature, the modern science, the modern public opinion; through their unearthly spirituality we are brought in near communion with the Divine ideas, and have no longer need of the anthropopathic mirror. Is this claim of superior holiness all false? is it so absurdly false, that the very statement, when distinctly made, must move wonder in those for whom it is offered?—then is the age not yet released from the study of the Scriptures, the very words and figures of the Scriptures. Then, instead of looking over these "accommodations," or looking under them, or pretending to *see through* them, must it be still our wisdom to sit down to the volume of revelation, and bring our heads and hearts in closest communion with this Divine language, until its hidden life-giving power shall flow over into our dead, dark, earthly souls.

Hence the plain position so essential to all earnest Biblical study, and which we have kept in view throughout this book. It is, that the very language of Scripture is specially, and most efficiently, designed for our moral and spiritual instruction. If it is *θεόπνευστος*, truly heaven-breathed, "then is it all profitable for teaching, for conviction, for correction, for education in righteousness." "Thy word, O Lord, is very pure, therefore thy servant loveth it." "Open thou mine eyes that I may behold wondrous things out of thy law." "The entrance of thy word giveth light, it giveth understanding." "The words that I speak unto you, they are spirit and they are life." The soul that feels this, and acknowledges this, has the ground of a true exegesis. Even the Neologists are very fond of calling the Bible Sacræ Scripturæ. One, the most commonly read of these commentators, is interpreting a Messianic psalm just as he would a Greek heroic song. In reproof of any contrary mode he very learnedly says—Quod antem in aliorum Scriptorum interpretatione omnes repudiarent, idem cur in *sacri codicis* explicatione admittatur, nullae idonea cogitari potest ratio—"No reason can be conceived why a mode which all reject in the interpretation of other writings should be admitted in the explanation of the *sacred text*." But what does he mean by his words *sacri codicis?* If it be indeed *sacra Scriptura*, sacred or *Holy Scripture*, then the very fact of its being such must make an immense difference between it and any Greek or Roman codex. To believe in his heart that it truly is *Sacred Scripture*, and that, therefore, every word of it is pure, every word of it holy (so far as we can hold it to be the genuine text or word of God), is the first great requisite of an interpreter. Without this idea, though the writing may be valuable and interesting in other respects, yet the laborious comment, which even the rationalists bestow upon it becomes a mockery and an absurdity. It is true, one cannot be a good interpreter, or the best interpreter, without linguistic and archæological knowledge. On the other hand, however, and with still greater boldness, may it be said of all Biblical interpretation that has not the unction of a hearty faith, that though it may be a blind aid to something higher than itself, yet in itself, and for itself, it is as worthless as "the sounding brass or the tinkling symbal." It is as dry, as light, as "the chaff of the summer threshing-floor." The wind shall drive it away. The onward march of the human mind shall consign it to oblivion. It shall have no lasting place, as a part either of secular or of sacred literature. The infidel and the believer shall alike scorn it. Neither in the world nor in the Church shall it ever have that post of honor which belongs to what is called genius in the one, or is prized as productive of holiness or spirituality in the other.

NOTES.

NOTE 1.—PAGE 65.

EXODUS, 33 : 20.—"*And he said, Thou canst not see my face, for no man can behold me and live. And the Lord said, There is a place by me, and thou shalt stand upon the rock, and it shall come to pass, when my glory passeth by, that I will put thee in the cleft of the rock, and I will cover thee with my hand and thou shalt see my back parts,* (את אחרי) *but my face cannot be seen.*" The divine *ahorim;* what are they but the aspect or side of deity that is turned to us, the rear shading of that ineffable mirror by which the divine glory is reflected to human eyes. They are the finities of the infinite, as the Hebrew word would seem to denote,—the side that is turned to human thought, and yet as real as that other which can never be seen by the finite eye or conceived by the finite understanding. The divine powers as seen in nature are also called קצות (Job. 26 : 14), or "*ends* of his ways," but it would seem to be his moral attributes that are here intended, although there was doubtless in the vision an outward glory. God passes by us in the scriptures as he passed by Moses "in the cleft of the rock," but it is his "goodness," his justice, his mercy, he proclaims, rather than that physical working which the pious naturalist might regard as the truer interpretation of the passage.

That which is infinite can have no finite: so says our piecemeal logic. But there is a higher power of the soul that comprehends, if it cannot analyze; that has an *idea*, if it cannot form a *conception*, or—if this is thought to be too boastful language—*believes*, where it cannot *understand*. The infinite contains the finite, must manifest the finite both in nature and revelation, must be able to think the finite, as a real divine thought, or it cannot be itself infinite, omniscient, almighty.

This two-fold aspect in the divine character appears in the very oldest scripture. The Spirit and the Word in creation, "the voice of Jehovah Elohim walking in Eden in the cool of the day;" how transcendent the ideas suggested by the one style of language, how human the conception presented in the other. The serious reader must have noted in other parts of the Pentateuch this remarkable union of the highest spirituality and the simplest anthropopathism, sometimes in almost immediate connection. The El Olam, the Eternal, the Almighty, the Most High, the same with the manifesting angel that wrestled with Jacob and talked so familiarly at the tent door with the pleading Patriarch,—the self-existent Jehovah, the ὁ ὤν, the "*I am that I am*," who immediately calls himself, in the next verse, a patrial God, "the God of Abraham, of Isaac, and of Jacob." In all such representations no contradiction is felt, none is expressed. God is the unrepresentable One (Deut. 4 : 15, 16), he has "no similitude;" and yet without any misgiving or sense of inconsistency there are ascribed to him acts and appearances, which, without the conception or imaging faculty, can have for us neither force nor meaning. In all this the writers must have seen the contrast, and yet these Old Scriptures go on their majestic way, neither calling attention to the divine height of the thought, nor ever apologizing for the human lowliness of the language and imagery.

NOTE 2.—PAGE 92.

ITS CRITICAL EDGE. The reference is to Hebrews, 4 : 12, where the Greek word κριτικὸς denotes the *separating* or analyzing power of the Logos, or the divine word *living* and energizing in the Scriptures. With this the whole imagery of that striking passage is in perfect harmony. "It is sharper than the two-edged sword,"—*διϊκνούμενος*, going clear through, penetrating to the very *cor*, core, or marrow of humanity. It *divides soul* and *spirit*, *ψυχή* and *πνεῦμα*. These words are not tautological repetitions employed for rhetorical intensity merely, neither are they designed to express a philosophical subtlety, but denote two departments of the inner man, most distinct, practically, in their workings, and most obvious, consciously, to those who make self-knowledge their deepest study. In one of these, namely, in the *ψυχή*, or sensitive nature, dwell what are, for the most part, the *motives* or moving powers of human action; whilst from the other, the *πνεῦμα*, or intellectual chamber, are brought the *reasons* by which we seek to disguise these moving powers, even from ourselves. We cannot bear our own sensual selfishness, and so this continual attempt,—for most men this life-long attempt,—to cover low *motives* with high *reasons*, is ever breeding a still greater darkness in the spirit. And so it goes on, until there comes the separating *word* making light, as of old it did upon the physical chaos; for *that* creation, too, was, in the main, a *dividing*, a critical separation of elements that before dwelt together in dark confusion. Another process of this critical word is to distinguish between the *ἐνθυμήσεις* and the *ἔννοιαι τῆς καρδίας*, "the thoughts and intents of the heart." This should be rendered rather the *thinkings* and the *thoughts*—the first referring to the actual present exercises or cogitations of the soul, which we suffer to become visible to ourselves; the other to the ἔννοιαι, the more interior principles, good or bad, the ruling ideas, or settled thoughts, that make the real man, though lying, it may be, long and far below the slumbering consciousness. The distinction, then, would be the same in both cases; and thus interpreting we see the force of the anatomical language that follows: "For all things lie naked and *dissected* (τετραχηλισμένα) before the eyes of him (or of that power), πρὸς ὃν ἡμῖν ὁ λόγος, to whom our discourse relates."

NOTE 3.—PAGE 94.

"*That I may apprehend that for which* (*or by which*) *I am apprehended of Christ Jesus*"—*Phil.* 3 : 12. The idea has given the commentators trouble, but the figure itself seems clear. It is an intense expression of that favorite thought of Paul, presented in the previous verse, of his intimate connection with Christ. If we take the metaphor in its more interior aspect, it is "having the mind of Christ" (*Phil.* 2 : 5); a knowing as he is known, an apprehending as he is apprehended. The more outward figure is in harmony with the τῆς ἄνω κλήσεως of the following verse, "the upward calling," or "calling upward." There is the same strong word διώκω in both clauses. "I press onward" toward him who is calling me upward, like the voice (Rev. 11 : 12) saying, ἀνάβητε ὧδε, "*Come up hither.*" It is a pressing upward to grasp him by whom he is grasped—to get a firm hold of a hand reached down from above; that hand which "lays hold of the seed of Abraham," ἐπιλαμβάνεται—*Heb.* 2 : 16. Some would refer it to Paul's conversion, or sudden *apprehension* by Christ, but this could be, in any case, only a part of the idea. If we choose thus to accommodate the language, it is admirably expressive of the Divine condescension or coming down to us, both in the incarnate and in the written word.

NOTE 4.—PAGE 106.

Heb. 9 : 1—Ἅγιον κοσμικὸν, "the *world-sanctuary*," or "*world-temple.*" The contrasts intended by the writer of Hebrews are so clear, that it is a wonder how commentators could have had any difficulty about the meaning of κοσμικὸν here, or how our translators could have so obscured the sense by rendering it "*worldly.*" The ἅγιον κοσμικὸν here is in contrast with the μείζονος καὶ τελειοτέρας σκηνῆς οὐ χειροποιήτου (verse 11), "the greater and more perfect tabernacle not made with hands," "where Christ, the High Priest, entered with his own blood, when he had found the *eternal* redemption." Compare with it, also, the ἅγια ἐπουράνια (verse 24), the "heavenly holies," or heaven itself, of which the *cosmical* holy was the type.

NOTE 5.—PAGE 139.

The passage is near the close of the VI Book of the Republic, 498 C. Socrates had been setting forth, at great length, the character of the "*true philosopher.*" Any one intimately acquainted with the Platonic writings knows how much the sense in which this word is employed transcends the use of it in any other writings, whether ancient or modern. No where else does the term *philosophy* come so near *religion.* The true philosopher, in the Platonic writings, is the man who, "unknown to the world" (see the Phædon, 64 A), or λεληθως τοὺς ἄλλους, lives for the *spiritual* and the *divine*, in distinction from the *sensual* and the *worldly.* He is one to whom there is, in some sense, a divine afflatus, ἔκ τινος θειάς ἐπιπνοίας ἀληθινῆς φιλοσοφίας ἀληθινὸς ἔρως, "a true love of true philosophy from some divine inbreathing." There could be no perfect commonwealth, it had been argued, until such philosophers had become its princes or magistrates. Was there anywhere such a State? Had there ever been a State so grounded on heavenly ideas, and a true Divine legislation? To these questions the answer is given: "If such a people so governed had ever existed in the immense past time, or if it now exists in some remote barbarian or foreign land, then are we prepared to maintain that our ideal State has been realized, or that it will be realized, whenever this Muse, *αὕτη ἡ Μοῦσα*, this philosophic inspiration, or heavenly philosophy, shall have become its ruling power. For the things of which we speak, though difficult, are not impossible." Plato was not a prophet, but who that reads this can avoid thinking of that divine or theocratic "polity" then actually existing in the barbarian land of Judea, and that then future polity of the Christian Church, of which it was ever the type? This was the Civitas Dei, and that true philosophy of which Plato dreamed, but could never see the accomplishment, even of his own very imperfect ideal.

NOTE 6.—PAGE 144.

We cannot easily believe Mohammed to have been a sheer impostor. The book he has given us has the style of high enthusiasm, far above that mere imitation aspect which characterizes most of the apocryphal Scriptures. He seems to have felt that he had a mission to restore the old patriarchal belief in the Divine Unity. He is, for the most part, in wonderful harmony with the Old Testament, and speaks not only with respect but tenderness of Jesus, conceding to him a position more divine than his own, and evidently regarding him as having had a divine and supernatural birth. Mohammed laid no claim to personal miracles, unless we regard as such his remarkable vision, and the maintenance of the inspiration of the Koran.

The great interest of this wonderful book, whose poetic form and nature are so little understood, consists in its independent narration of some of the leading events in the early Old Testament history. We cannot here state the argument, but there is abundant internal evidence that the stories of Abraham, of Noah, of Joseph, of Ishmael, together with other ancient events not mentioned in the Jewish Scriptures, such as the accounts of the prophets Hud and Saleh, were not derived from the Bible, but came down from independent collateral tradition among these sons of the desert; and that these traditions date away back to the times of Ishmael, and even to Joktan, who was the son of Eber the great ancestor both of the Jews and the Arabians.

NOTE 7.—PAGE 155.

"*Held sacred from a long antiquity.*" See Josephus, *Antiq.*, *Book II.*, *Chap.* 12. When speaking of Sinai, he says: "Now this is the highest of all the mountains thereabouts, and the best for pasturage, the herbage there being good; but it had not been before fed upon, because of the opinion men had that God dwelt there, the shepherds not daring to ascend up to it." We learn, too, from other sources, that this whole region of desert country, from the northern extremity all the way down the east side of the Arabian Gulf or the Red Sea, had a religious veneration attached to it. It had sacred places, and a *religio loci*, and consecrated shrines, from a great antiquity. See Diodorus Siculus iii., 42. From this source probably came that early veneration of the *Kaaba*, or shrine of Mecca, of which Mohammed makes so much account. Such veneration may have had its origin in the weird aspect of these singular regions, but this idea does not detract from the inspiration of the narrative in Exodus. God may have chosen to meet his servant there on that very account. Or the story of the ancient supernatural may have been a subsequent tradition, growing out of that feeling which naturally connects a *religio loci* with any great event, religious or historical. Such is the tradition to which Virgil refers in regard to the site of early Rome, when Evander leads Æneas to the site of the Tarpeian rock and the seat of the Capitol that afterwards, for so long a time, had a religious veneration in Roman history, and which, even yet, maintains its power over the souls of men.

Hinc ad Tarpeiam sedem et Capitolia ducit
Aurea nunc, olim sylvestribus horrida dumis.
Jam tum *religio* pavidos terrebat agrestes
Dira loci; jam tum sylvam saxumque tremebant.
Hoc nemus, hunc, inquit, frondoso vertice, collem,
Quis Deus incertum est, habitat Deus. Arcades ipsum
Credunt se vidisse Jovem ; cum sæpe nigrantem
Ægida concuteret dextra, nimbosque cieret.

ÆNEID, VIII., 347.

NOTE 8.—PAGE 257.

It may seem strange that the perfect adaptedness of this 88th Psalm to the condition of the leper king, Uzziah, should have escaped the notice of commentators; and yet we cannot help being impressed by it. "And Uzziah the king was a leper unto the day of his death, and he dwelt in a *free house* (or separate house), being a leper; for he was cut off from the house of the Lord; and Jotham, his son, was over the king's house, judging the people of the land."—2 Chron., 26 : 12.

One of the most striking coincidences, philologically, between this passage and the Psalm referred to, is found in the Hebrew word חפשי, which, although of rather rare occurrence elsewhere, occurs in both these places, and with a remarkable similarity of idea. The primary sense of the word is *free.* As the derivative is used in 2 Chronicles, 26 : 21, it denotes a *free house*, in the sense of a person left to himself, *immu-*

nis, away from ordinary employments, separate, alone. There is a similar use of the Latin *liber*, as in the phrase *liberæ ædes*, a dwelling occupied by no one else. Most impressively corresponding to this is the use of the word, Ps. 88 : 6 : "*Free among the dead;*" or, as the Syriac version renders it, "A freed man in the house of the dead."

Now, remembering that Uzziah had been a religious king, notwithstanding this act of impiety, let us compare with the history the language of the Psalm. Can we find anything that so exactly fits it, whether we regard its exact description, its strong suggestiveness of similar ideas, or its most touching pathos?

> Lord God of my salvation,
> Day and night my cry is before thee.
> Let my prayer come unto thee ;
> Incline thine ear to my wailing.
> For my soul is full of sorrow ;
> My life draws nigh to Sheol.
> *Free among the dead,*
> Like the slain, like the sleepers in the grave,
> Whom thou rememberest no more,
> Who are cut off from thy hand.

That is, from thy worship; they come no more into the house of the Lord, as we are told in Chronicles—"For he was cut off from the house of the Lord."

> Thou hast laid me in the lowest pit,
> In the darkness, in the shadowy depths.
> *Thou hast put far from me my familiar friends,*
> *Thou hast made me a loathing to them.*

The language following we cannot help regarding as that of soliloquy rather than despair. It seems the rising of a faint hope, presenting itself in the form of wondering query, like Job's exclamation: "If a man die shall he really live again?" So here there would seem such a ray of consolation feebly entering this dark house of death. It is the rising thought of some possible higher life, yet barely strong enough to call out the musing soliloquizing style. As though he had asked himself, in wonder at the very conception, "Ah! can it be?"

> Wilt thou work a miracle for the dead?
> Shall the ***Rephaim*** (the manes) rise up and praise thee?
> Shall, indeed, thy mercy be told in the grave?
> Thy faithfulness in Abaddon?
> Shall thy wonder be really known in the darkness,
> Thy righteousness in the Land of Oblivion?

And then a more assuring strain. The soul seems to rise out of its darkness:

> And yet, O Lord, my cry is unto thee;
> In the *morning* shall my prayer still come before thee;
> For why, Jehovah, wouldst thou cast off my soul?
> Why hide thy face from me?

Is the *morning* here the morning of a new life? There are some passages in the Psalms that would seem to warrant such an interpretation. In the closing lines, however, there returns again the gloom of the prison-house:

Wretched am I and spent with trembling;
I bear thy terrors,—I am wild with sorrow.
Thy wrath passes over me,—thy alarms consume me;
They come round me like floods all the day.
Far from me hast thou put lover and friend,
My nearest ones are away from my darkness.

There is but one thing that would seem in the least inconsistent with such a view. It is the expression, v. 15, "*from my youth up*," as it is rendered in our common version. But the root there found, when used for *youth*, is almost every where else in the plural, like the corresponding Hebrew term for age. The two or three cases where it seems to have that sense in the singular, do all admit of a better, though a kindred version. Its root sense (*agitation*) is the one here employed; as Psalms 109 : 23.

On farther examination, we find that a similar view of the Psalm is taken by Ikenius, and combated by Venema. See *Venema on the Psalms*, vol. 5, p. 69.

NOTE 9.—PAGE 279.

The reference is to Isaiah 45 : 7. "I am the Lord; and there is no other. I form the light and create darkness; I make peace and create evil." Formans *lucem* et creans *tenebras*, faciens pacem et creans *malum*. The best commentators have regarded it as directed against the Persian or ancient Oriental doctrine of the *two principles*, *good* and *evil*, or *light* and *darkness*, as taught in the Zendavesta. It was employed also by the Fathers against the heretic Marcion, who held the same opinion.

NOTE 10.—PAGE 281.

The Vulgate gives us a very singular rendering of this passage—" *Gloria in altissimis Deo, et in terra pax hominibus bonæ voluntatis;*" " *Glory to God in the highest, and on earth peace to men of good-will.*" In this it is followed by the Rheims and Wickliffe translations that were made from it. It requires the Greek reading εὐδοκίας which has little or no authority. Every critical reader must see how it mars the glorious passage. Indeed, it is one of the most serious faults of this, in the main, admirable version of the Scriptures.

NOTE 11.—PAGE 351.

In Isaiah 24 : 5, the Jews are charged with having broken the "*Everlasting Covenant,*" ברית עולם. But what is meant by this? Aben Esra regards it as the universal unwritten law of nature and conscience. To the same effect is it interpreted by Hieronymus. But Gesenius maintains—and justly, we think—that such an idea is alien to the Jewish mind, accustomed as it was from the beginning to precise mandates and national stipulations. The high sense, however, which the prophet evidently intended, is found (and that, too, in strictest harmony with the national ideas) in this "Old Covenant," which made the Jews a *world-people*, as we have called then, and gave them a *world-destiny*. See *Deut.* 32 : 8. It was the promise to Abraham (and that, too, a clearer republication of the promise in Eden), that "in his seed all the nations of the earth should be blessed;" in other words, that in the line of his seed should come the Seed of the woman, the anciently-promised Redeemer or Deliverer of mankind. This was the *Berith Olam*, *διαθήκη αἰωνίος*, *foedus sempiternum*, the Covenant of Eternity, the *world-covenant*, the covenant that, transcending their local history in Palestine, was to go through the *ages*, or olams, carrying out the great idea on which the Jews, obscurely as they may have understood it, ever prided themselves. "Israel was," in some way, to be "God's salvation, even to the ends of the earth." Even in the more restricted sense it was a "covenant of ages." The national Israel survived the Assyrian, the Persian, the Greek, and Macedonian empires. But its highest fulfilment is in that "true Israel," or *Civitas Dei*, to which all other nations and all other history have been, and ever will be, subservient.

www.ingramcontent.com/pod-product-compliance
Lightning Source LLC
LaVergne TN
LVHW020106110826
845151LV00001B/81

* 9 7 8 1 4 2 5 5 4 4 4 5 4 *